American Airborne Pathfinders

American Airborne Pathfinders
in World War II

Jeff Moran

Schiffer Military History
Atglen, PA

Acknowledgments

First and foremost I would like to thank the veterans who shared their experiences and knowledge. This book would not have been possible without their assistance. This book is as much theirs as it is mine. I would also like to especially thank Mark Bando, Michel De Trez, and Bill Rentz, all three historians and collectors for many years, for their generosity and support in providing many of the photographs in this book. Their wealth of knowledge has been truly appreciated. I am also grateful to George Koskimaki for his generosity in sharing his vast research on the 101st Airborne Division during the war. I wish to thank my father, James Moran, who encouraged me to complete my research and make my book a reality. My thanks goes out to everyone who contributed to my research for this book:

Contributors

Jim Allardyce
Berge Avadanian
Mark Bando
Dave Berry
Dudley Cone
Michel De Trez
Henry Filipczak
Howard W. Hicks
Les Hughes
Jerome V. Huth
Curtis Gadd
John Gerard
Thomas L. Jones
Arnold Justice
Melissa Kramer
George Koskimaki
William Lumsden
MacLean Lunko
Jim McNamara
Dan Morgan
Robert M. Murphy
Cheryl Nolin
Jack Norton
Ben Overhand
Charles Petty
Beul E. Putnam
Bill Rentz
Greg Russell
Roy Smith
Jeff Warner

Dedication

This book is dedicated to the Pathfinders and all other soldiers, men and women alike who honorably served our country in the past, present, and future.

Soldier

I was that which others did not want to be, and I went where
others feared to go. I did what others failed to do. I asked nothing from
those who gave nothing, and reluctantly
accepted the thought of eternal loneliness ... should I fail.
I have seen the face of terror; felt the stinging cold of fear, and
enjoyed the sweet taste of a moment's love. I have cried,
pained, and hoped ... But most of all, I have lived times others
would say were best forgotten. At least someday, I will be able
to say that I was proud of what I was ...

- A Soldier

Book design by Robert Biondi.

Library of Congress Catalog Number: 2002115967.

Printed in China.
ISBN: 0-7643-1769-5

Published by Schiffer Publishing Ltd.
4880 Lower Valley Road
Atglen, PA 19310
Phone: (610) 593-1777
FAX: (610) 593-2002
E-mail: Info@schifferbooks.com.
Visit our web site at: www.schifferbooks.com
Please write for a free catalog.
This book may be purchased from the publisher.
Please include $3.95 postage.
Try your bookstore first.

In Europe, Schiffer books are distributed by:
Bushwood Books
6 Marksbury Ave.
Kew Gardens
Surrey TW9 4JF
England
Phone: 44 (0)20 8392-8585
FAX: 44 (0)20 8392-9876
E-mail: Bushwd@aol.com.
Free postage in the UK. Europe: air mail at cost.
Try your bookstore first.

Contents

Foreword

The concept of the parachute and men dropping from the sky may have had its origins in ancient times. Later, Leonardo da Vinci during the fifteenth century illustrated plans for a parachute for such a purpose. During the 1930s the Soviet Union developed plans for the use of parachute troops and trained a group of soldiers to jump from airplanes.

It was not until the Second World War that the idea of soldiers jumping from the sky was used in a practical and mass scale with the development of the airborne forces. Aircraft were designed or modified for the purpose of carrying airborne soldiers. Equipment was developed to meet the special needs of these soldiers, and training and tables of organization were developed.

The United States formed five Airborne Divisions during the war: the 11th, 13th, 17th, 82nd, and 101st. The men from these airborne divisions participated in some of the most memorable actions of the Second World War. In 1943 the 82nd Airborne Division jumped into Sicily. Both the 82nd and 101st jumped into Normandy in the invasion of Northwest Europe. In an attempt to put Allied troops across the Rhine River both the 82nd and 101st participated in Operation Market Garden along with airborne forces of Great Britain. The 101st participated in the epic defense of Bastogne, Belgium during the Battle of the Bulge in December 1944. Operation Varsity, saw the use of the 17th Airborne Division in a drop across the Rhine.

The earliest use of American airborne forces during World War II was in a jump into North Africa. The troops were scattered over a wide area. In 1943 there was the drop of paratroopers during the invasion of Sicily. Again there was wide scattering of troops. In August 1943, training started for operators of Eureka radars – these men were given the designation 'Pathfinders'. Their mission was to jump into enemy held territory prior to the main airborne landing and serve as guides for the remainder of the airborne assault.

First use of the newly formed pathfinders was in a drop during the Salerno landings in Italy. Trained in the use of the Eureka radar, holophan lights, and colored ground panels the pathfinders dropped thirty minutes before the main airborne landing to provide ground guidance for successive airborne jumps. The concept of the pathfinders proved successful and they were used during the remainder of the Second World War.

In this book, Jeff Moran tells the story of the Pathfinders and the vital part they played in airborne operations during the Second World War. He has told the story of the operations they led, the equipment that was often unique and used by them and has memorialized them by noting in many cases the individual teams of pathfinders. Whether a student of airborne history or a collector of airborne artifacts this book will be of interest to the reader and contribute to our understanding and appreciation of this part of our military history.

James Moran
November 2002

Introduction

Early in World War II the U.S. Army developed airborne units that would parachute behind enemy lines to accomplish various missions. It was quickly learned that in order to drop large airborne units accurately a small group of paratroops was needed to guide the airborne divisions to their assigned drop zones and glider landing zones.

In 1942, the 82nd Airborne Division and 509th Parachute Infantry Battalion began to experiment with this new concept. Within a few months the 'Pathfinders' emerged. These volunteers received special training for the hazardous duties they would perform. They would spearhead the airborne assaults in small groups of eighteen men or less to set up special equipment to aid pilots of the Troop Carrier Command to navigate to designated drop zones.

During the war nearly one-thousand pathfinders were trained from the various airborne units and they participated in nearly every major airborne operation. Since World War II, pathfinders have performed their mission in the Korean, Vietnam, and Gulf Wars. During the Vietnam War specific 'Pathfinder' detachments and companies were organized into units to perform their mission rather than ad hoc units brought together for single operations. They continue to be a valuable asset in the U.S. Army today.

I believe this is the first book written entirely about the American Pathfinders during World War II. I wrote this to preserve a small but important portion of our military history for generations to come. What began so many years ago has continued and evolved in today's armies throughout the world. The Army's current Pathfinder School at Fort Benning, Georgia still teaches the same basic techniques taught more than a half century ago. Graduates of the school continue to be awarded the distinction of wearing the flaming winged torch.

Jeff Moran
November 2002

Chapter One

SPECIAL EQUIPMENT

Eureka Beacon AN/PPN-1A and Rebecca Receiver APN-2 (SCR-729)

The transmitter beacon AN/PPN-1A, known as Eureka was a British designed and manufactured radar device inspired by General F.A.M. Browning. Once built, the honor of naming them went to Browning. "Eureka", is the Greek word meaning, "I found it"! It was also manufactured later in the United States. It was a 75-pound man-pack radar beacon, carried by a single pathfinder on the jump and set up on the drop zone for the transport aircraft to home in on. It was used with a counterpart, Rebecca, located in the C-47 aircraft. Browning chose the name "Rebecca" as his wife was novelist Daphne du Maurier, *Rebecca* being the title of her most popular book.

The Eureka could transmit on five frequencies and receive on five additional frequencies. Rebecca transmitted on Eureka's frequency and received on its transmitting frequency. By planned allocations of frequencies, it was possible to identify the correct Eureka for each aircraft's DZ. On receiving the impulse from the aircraft's Rebecca, the Eureka on the DZ replied automatically. From Rebecca the aircraft navigator could read off his distance from the DZ and his compass bearing to it.

Since there was some danger of too many aircraft flying to one DZ guiding on the Eureka, Rebeccas were only to be used by group and flight leaders and any pilots who lost formation. On the ground pathfinders were instructed to switch on their Eurekas only fifteen minutes before the main body of aircraft were due to arrive and switch it off twenty minutes after the main drop. There was no provision for radio voice connection between the aircraft and the DZ.

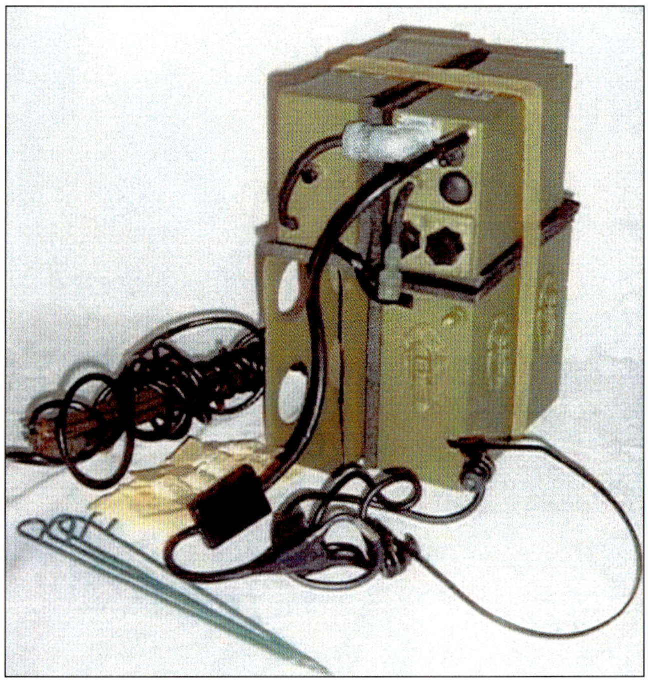

AN/PPN-1A Eureka Beacon. *Courtesy of Jeff Warner*

The Eureka had a built-in self-destruct explosive device which could be detonated by pulling a pin. This device was to help ensure that the top-secret Eureka wouldn't fall into enemy hands.

Each pathfinder team would be equipped with two Eurekas with each Eureka having an assigned operator and an assistant operator. The Eureka beacon was first used in 1942 by the 509th PIR in North Africa, but not by pathfinders.

A special bag was designed at Newbury, Berkshire, England by the Independent Paratroops Company, 101st Airborne Division, to carry the Eureka beacon set. The bag was made by the S. Froehlich Co. Inc., of New York City in 1944. It was made of a tan waterproof cloth lined with felt and closed with a heavy zipper. It had an outside compartment for carrying a folding antenna.

A special harness made of parachute webbing was made by riggers to carry the bag during the jump and after landing, and made the bag easier to carry as a back pack.

Destruction button on the Eureka Beacon. *Courtesy of Jeff Warner*

Another view of the Eureka Beacon. *Courtesy of Jeff Warner*

View of the frequency meter controls. *Courtesy of Jeff Warner*

Eureka beacon carrying case made by the S. Froehlich Co., Inc. in New York City. Two variations of makers stamps are known, all being dated 1944. *Author's Collection*

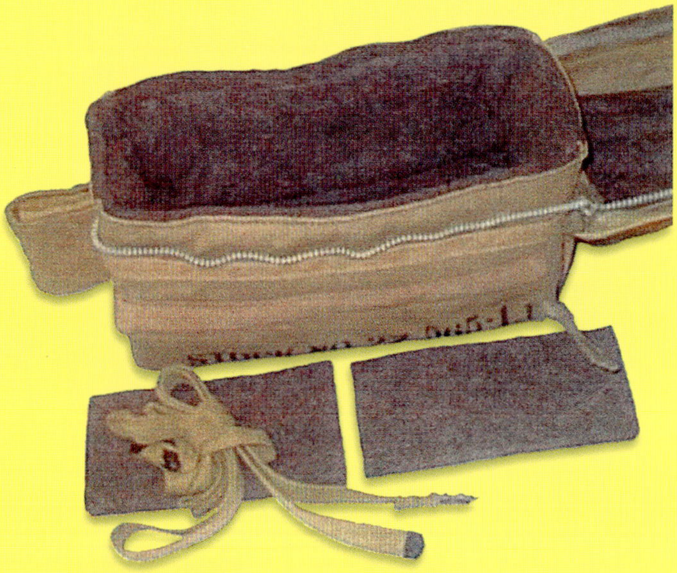

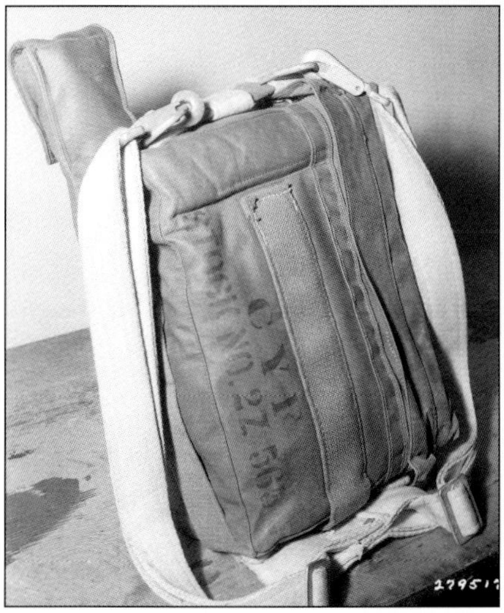

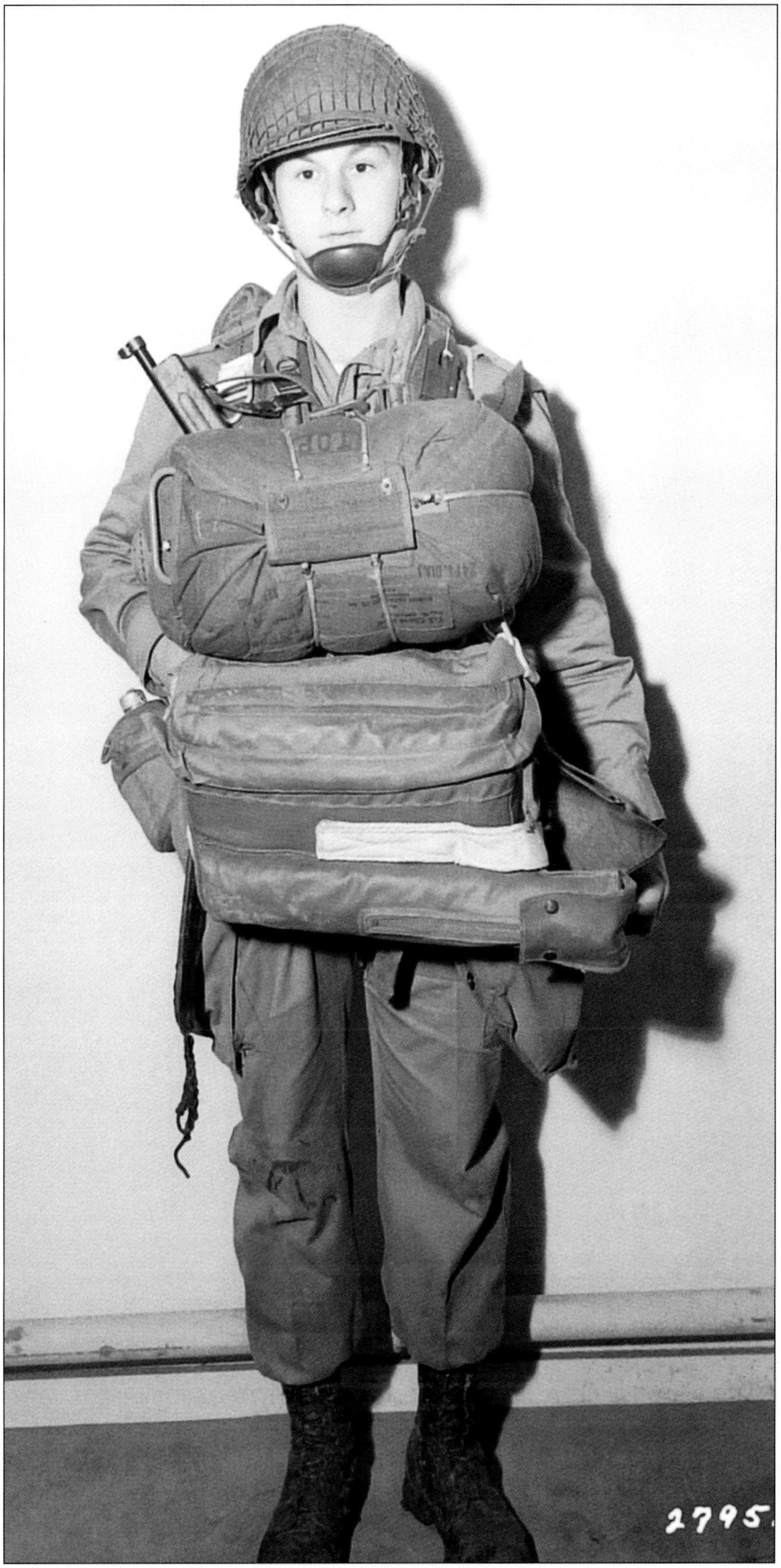

Above and right: Rigger made harness to carry the Eureka case. *Courtesy U.S. Army*

Below: An unknown troop carrier pilot. Note the Rebecca antenna on the side of the aircraft, a second antenna was also on the opposite side. *Author's Collection*

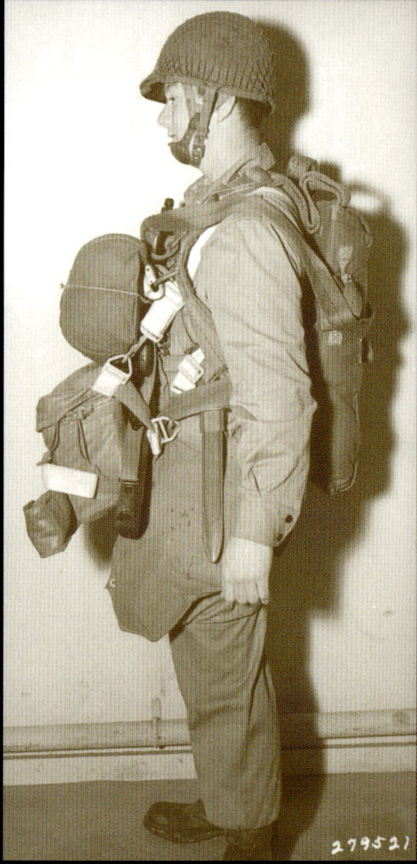

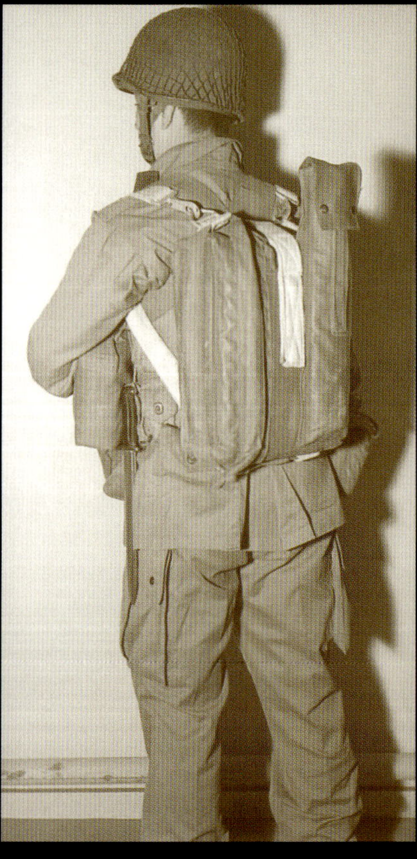

Three views of a pathfinder demonstrating the wear of the Eureka case below his reserve parachute and on his back. *Courtesy of the National Archives*

A pathfinder exiting the aircraft with a Eureka Beacon. *Courtesy of Michel De Trez*

Eureka Beacon AN/PPN-2

Later in 1944 a second model of the Eureka beacon the RT-37/AN/PPN-2 was manufactured in the United States. It was a very different design being smaller with fewer components and lighter in weight. It was 9_ in. long and 14_ in. wide and weighed only 28 pounds. This model too was equipped with an internal self-destruct device and was also carried in a waterproof canvas carrying case. The instruction manuals, antenna with guy lines and pegs were carried inside the case. The twenty-five foot extension cable however was tied to the outside of the case. This cable allowed the range of the beacon to be increased from fifteen to fifty miles according to the aircraft's altitude.

The components of the PPN-2 Eureka beacon consisted of the set itself, AS-73/PPN-2 antenna, extension cable, three guy lines, three stakes, HS-30 headset, TM11-1145 instruction manual and instruction cards, and MX-183/PPN-2 padded carrying case. It was powered by a BB 212/U battery

The PPN-2 beacons were only used during Operation Varsity in March 1945.

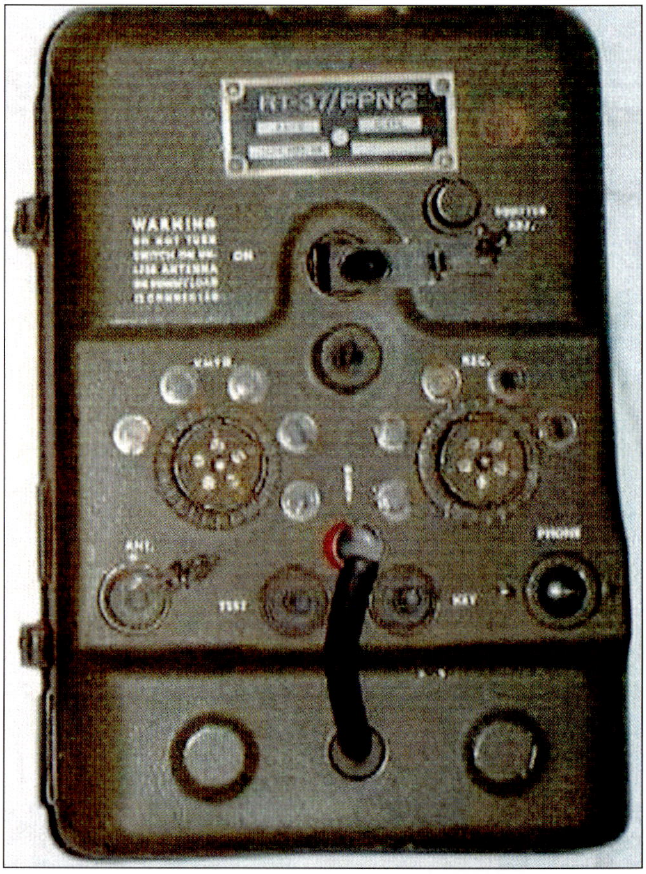

Top right: AN/PPN-2 Eureka Beacon. *Courtesy of James Bell* Bottom right: Under side of the beacon, notice the design to help with the destruction of the device. *Courtesy of James Bell* Below: TM 11-1145 Manual for the Eureka Beacon. *Courtesy of James Bell*

5G Radio Transmitter Beacon

Weighed thirty-three pounds.

GEE TR1335

The GEE was a British radio system based on triangulation. The name GEE came from the first letter in the word 'Grid' and was installed in all pathfinder C-47 transports. The GEE would receive radio pulses transmitted from three separate stations in England. The signals received by means of a CRT (cathode-ray tube) were checked by the navigator on board the aircraft against a specially prepared map of lattice lines covering all of Northwest Europe within one hundred miles of the English coast.

GEE was effective at distances over 100 miles, and the IX Troop Carrier Command estimated its accuracy at 400 yards under ideal conditions.

GEE TR1335. *Author's Collection*

SCR-717

The SCR-717 was an American S-band search radar fitted in the lead aircraft. It was a primitive form of scanner, which could show on a screen in the aircraft a rough outline of the landscape below by reflecting water as black and land and shipping as white. A few responder sets, called BUPs, which could produce a bright spot on the SCR-717 screen, were also issued to pathfinders.

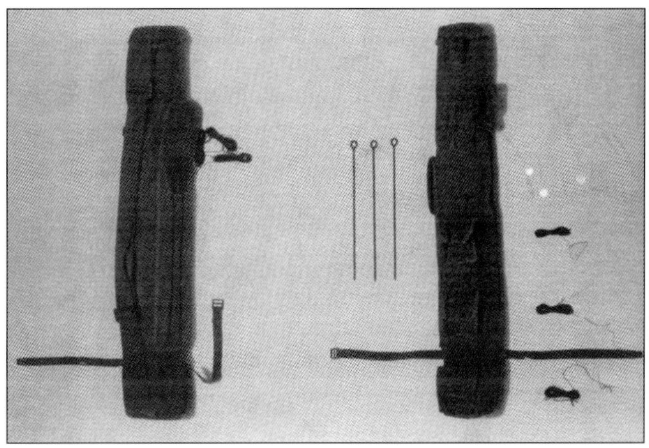

AN/UPN-1 BUPs Beacon carrying case. *Courtesy of Michel De Trez*

BUPs (AN/UPN-1) Radar Beacon

The BUPs radar beacon responder set worked with the SCR-717. It sent out an ultra-high frequency radio wave signal that flashed bright blips on the SCR-717 screen. The 110-pound set was developed by the British Branch Radiation Laboratories specifically for the pathfinders. One member of each division was tasked with carrying the beacon and was used as the center navigational point for each division.

It consisted of a unit mounted on top of a telescopic antenna pole, three guy cords, and carrying case. The set was

Left: A pathfinder of the Airborne Command with the BUPs beacon. *Author's Collection*

carried in a waterproof bag that could be attached to the pathfinder during the jump.

During the Normandy invasion the 101st Airborne's BUPs beacon made it to DZ 'C' but was inoperative (antenna was broken on landing). The 82nd Airborne's beacon was apparently lost.

M/F Beacon

Long wave radio transmitter that worked in tandem with radio compasses.

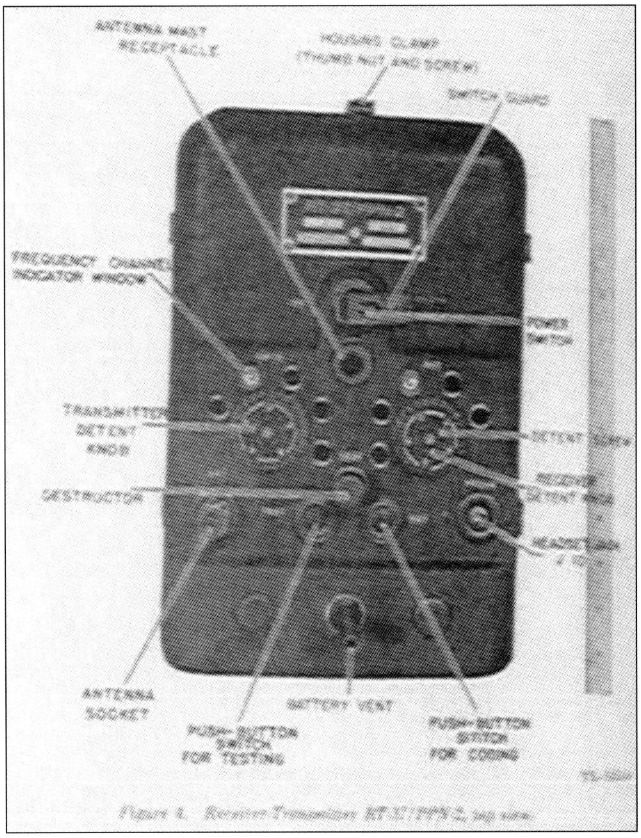

Above and right: Three pages of the manual showing the use of the beacon, controls of the beacon, and fully assembled beacon. *Courtesy of James Bell*

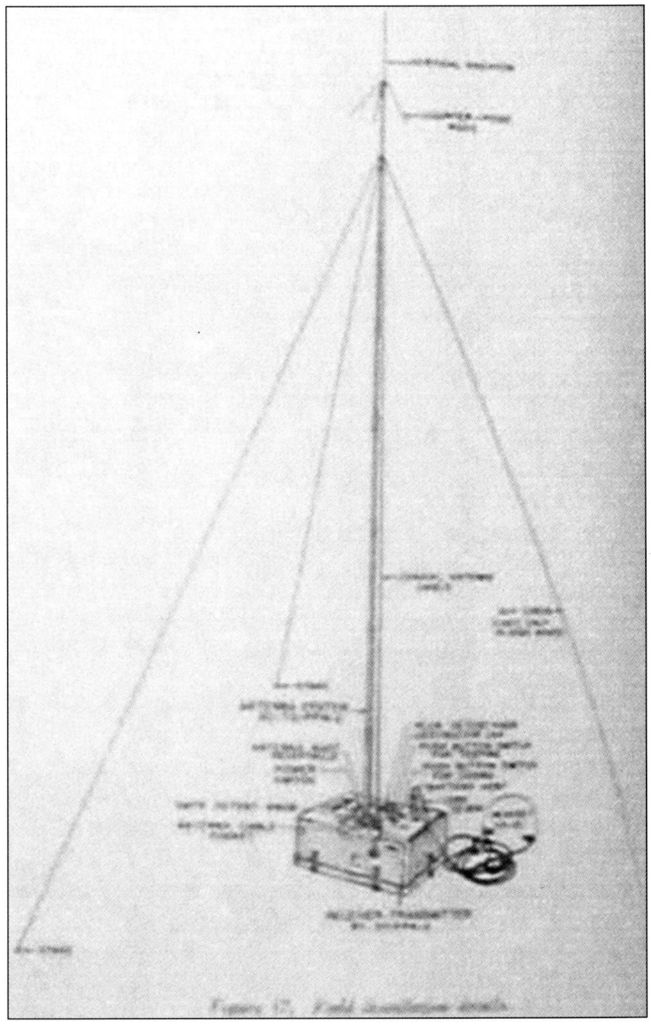

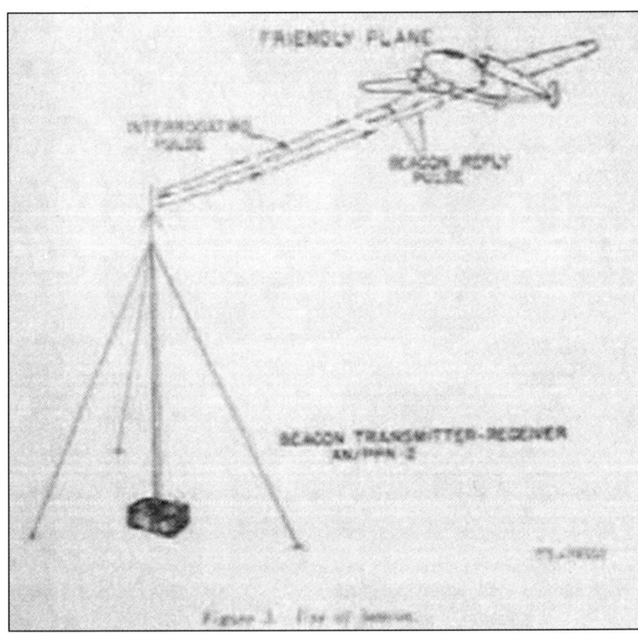

Holophane (Halifane) Light

Holophane lights were mounted on a wooden adjustable tripod that stood about five feet tall. The three legs could each be extended twice by means of tightening screws. The tripod could be leveled by means of a double spirit level set in its head. Atop the tripod the light was attached by means of a tightening screw. The lights could be changed from various colors; red, green, amber, or yellow. During the Normandy operation each DZ and LZ was designated by a different color. The light attachments were carried in a small wooden box. They were powered by six volt (car) battery and operated by a telegraph key on a twenty-five foot extension cable. The lights were carried in pairs in the B-3 case. The case was strapped by a rigger made harness to the parachute harness and attached just below the reserve parachute. A special canvas case was made by the riggers for the battery to be carried separately during the jump.

Each pathfinder stick was to carry eight lights, seven for the 'T' and one for reserve. For the Normandy invasion the colors designated for the drop zones were green for DZs 'A' and 'N', red for DZs 'C' and 'O', and amber for DZs 'D' and 'T'.

Pvt. Clark a British pathfinder putting into operation a Holophane light. *Courtesy Michel De Trez*

Below: B3 case for carrying the Holophane light with rigger made harness. *Courtesy of the National Archives*

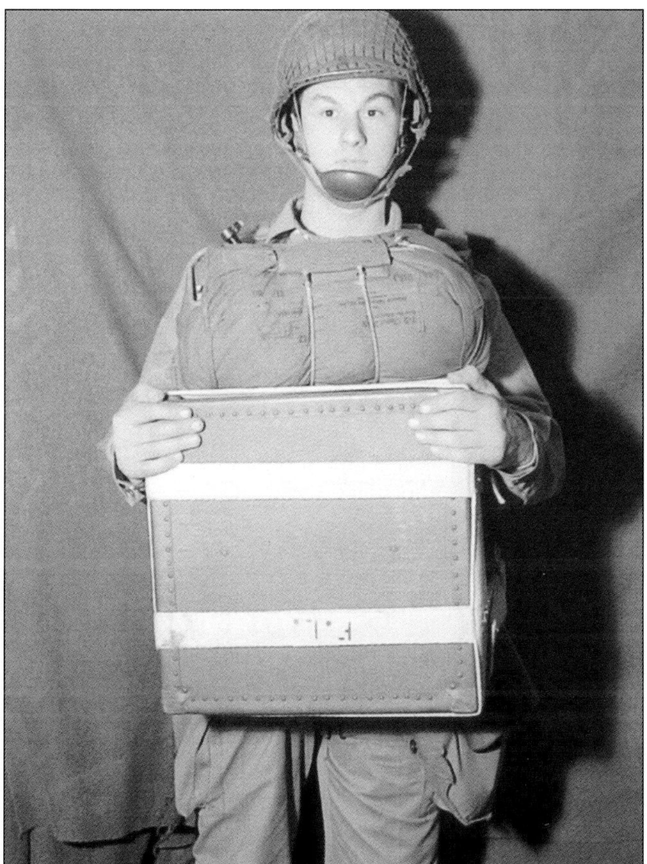

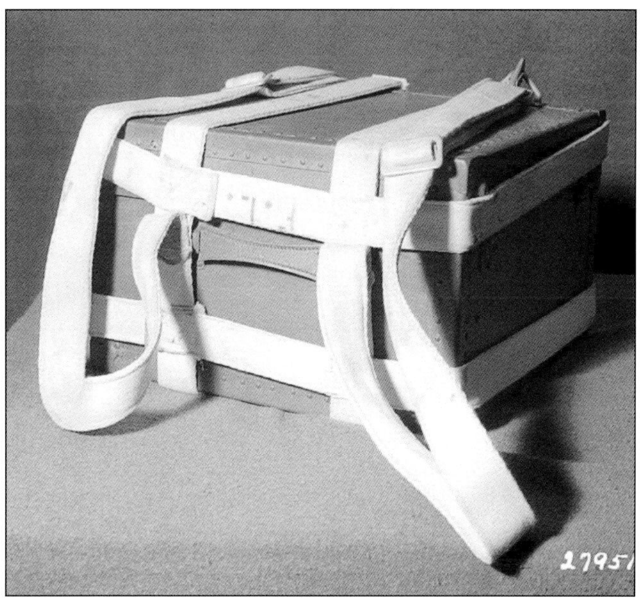

Left and pages 20-21: Three views of a pathfinder demonstrating the wear of the B3 Holophane light case. *Courtesy of the National Archives*

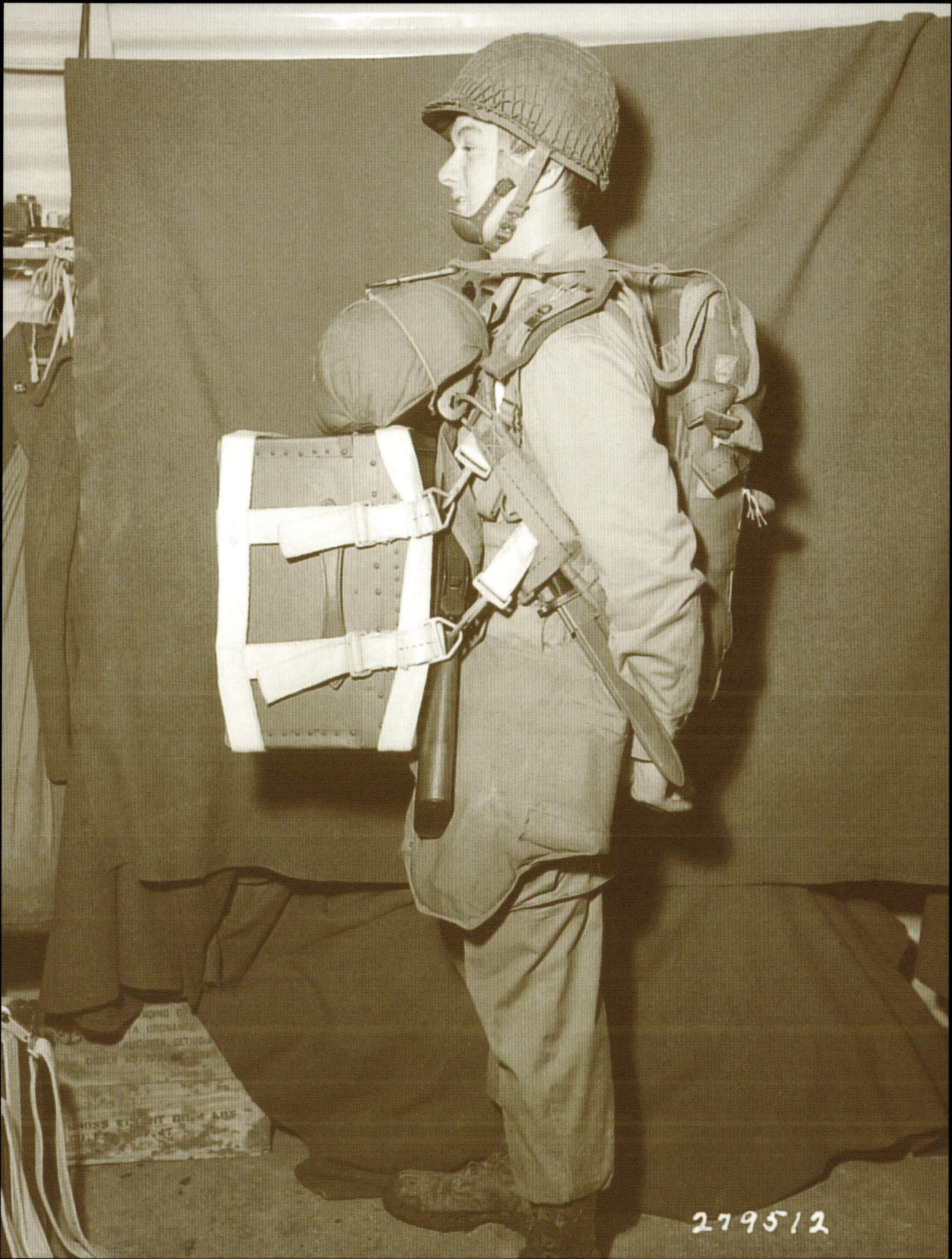
279512

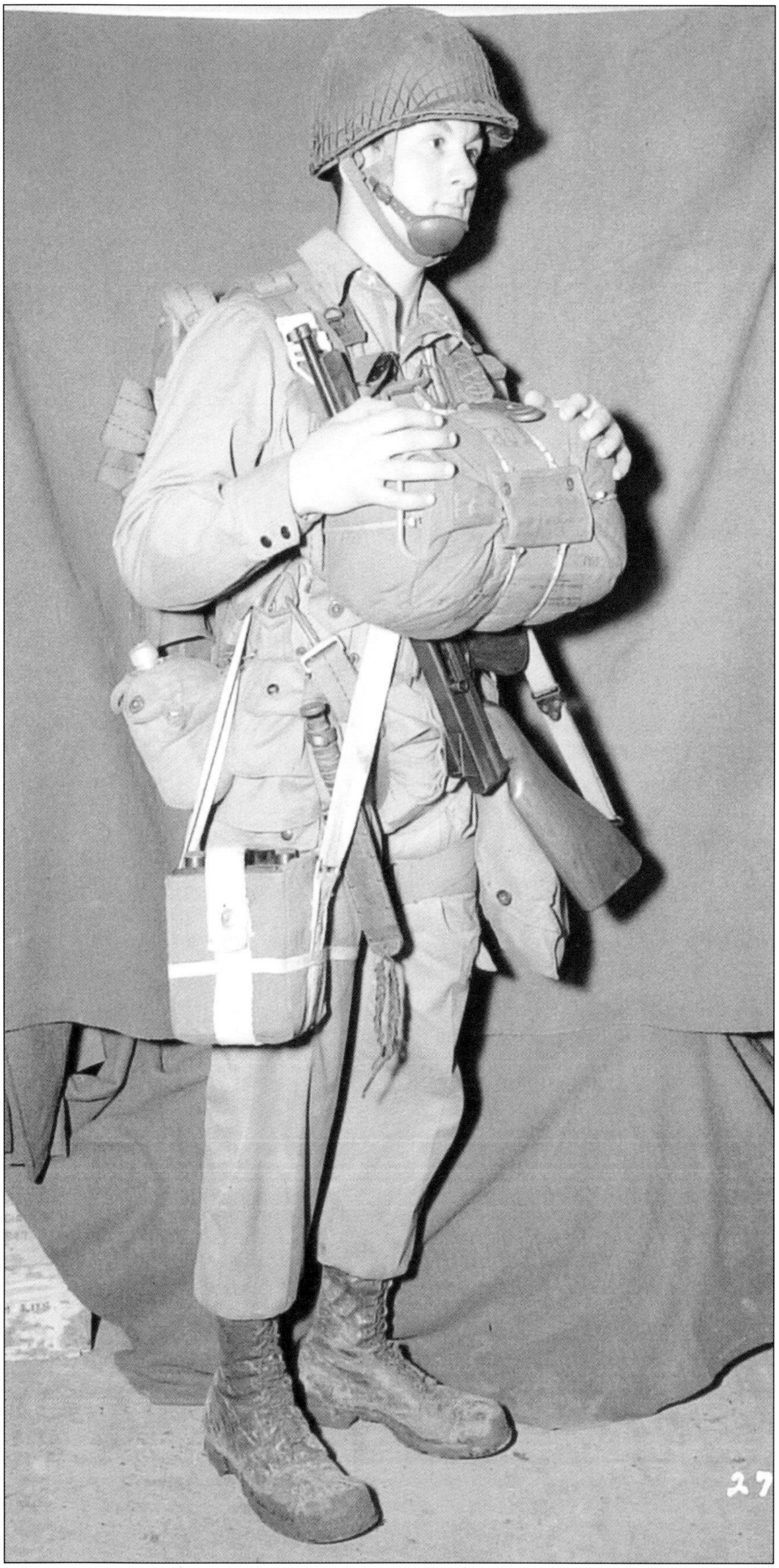

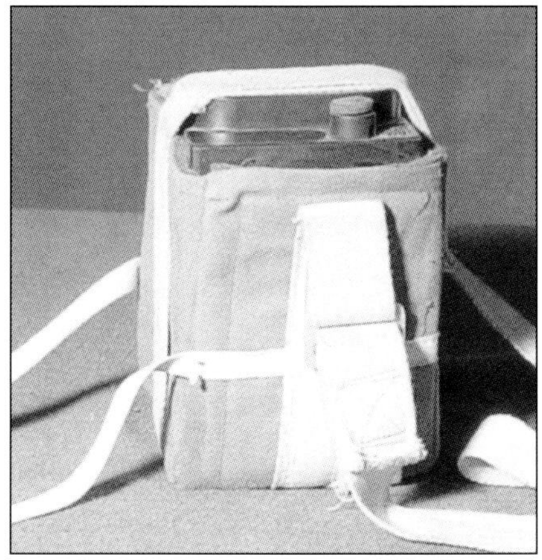

Above: Battery for the Holophane light with rigger made carrying case. *Courtesy of the National Archives*

Left: A pathfinder demonstrating the wear of the battery for the Holophane light. *Courtesy of the National Archives*

Below: A pathfinder lieutenant of the 101st Airborne Division with an Aldis Lamp Case below his reserve parachute. *Courtesy of Mark Bando*

Aldis Light

The Aldis light is a high-intensity flashlight with a very narrow, directional beam. It was used to relay signals throughout flights as serials approached the drop zones or landing zones. The light was initially flashed by the radio operators of the lead aircraft, and relayed throughout the formation. A red light signaled the prescribed time from the jump or the glider release. The lens was then changed and a green light signaled the jump release.

Aldis Lights were also used by the paratroop pathfinders on several operations during the war.

Below: Aldis Light with case, power cord, and red and blue lenses. Right: Closer view of the Aldis light. *Author's Collection*

Kryton Light

Battery operated.

M-227 Signal Lamp

The M-227 (SE-11) Signal lamp is a portable field signaling device for transmitting messages by means of white or red flashes of light in International Morse Code. It operates by the use of five BA-30 dry cell batteries. It is designed for three methods of operation; as a gun, remote control off a tripod from fifteen feet away by a hand key, or from a half mile away by means of telephone wire and hand key.

The signal lamp was developed in early 1943 and manufactured by nine companies. It was issued with a carrying bag (BG-131) and various accessories.

M-227 Signal Lamp with carrying bag and accessories. *Author's Collection*

AL-140-B Signal Panel

The AL-140-B signal panel is a rectangular cloth panel twelve feet by 30.5 inches wide, with a bright red, orange, or yellow pliable plastic sheeting on one side and gloss white on the other. The panel could be fixed to the ground by straps around its edge. The panel is rolled from its free end and then secured in its attached khaki colored carrying case. This case is kept secured by means of a press-studs so as to avoid accidental unrolling. Three 'lift-the-dot' press fasteners fasten and fully close the large flap. An adjustable cloth strap allows the case to be carried over the shoulder.

These panels were used to mark DZs and LZs for daylight operations. They were used with two or more being arranged on the ground to form designated letters or symbols to signify re-supply, wind direction, hostile forces direction, or drop or landing zones.

Three panels could be carried in a special canvas case, the CS-150R. Two versions of this case are known; one U.S. made with snaps and the other was British made with straps and buckles.

Al-140-B Signal Panel. *Author's Collection*

Bright red signal panel (left), Case CS-150R (top right) and experimental signal panel carrying case dated 1941 (bottom right) for carrying three signal panels. *Author's Collection*

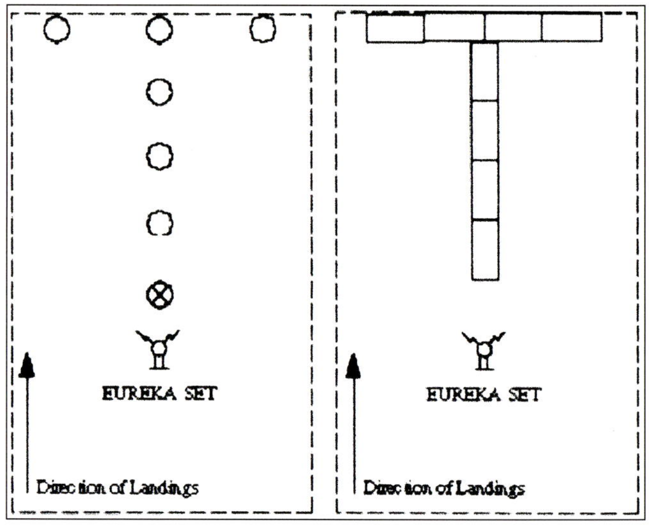

Illustrations showing pathfinders laying out a signal panel, and 'T' placement of lights and signal panels. *Courtesy of Michel De Trez*

Delta Lantern

Used to mark glider LZs at night in Normandy.

Delta Lantern with carrying case (general purpose bag). *Author's Collection*

'Keeler Light'

The Keeler Light was invented by Lt. Keeler of the 505th Para Inf. Regt., 82nd Abn. Div. for the Salerno operation. As S/Sgt. Berge Avadanian of the 505th recalls, "it was basically a broomstick like pole with a #10 food can with a flashlight in it which could only be seen from the incoming planes."

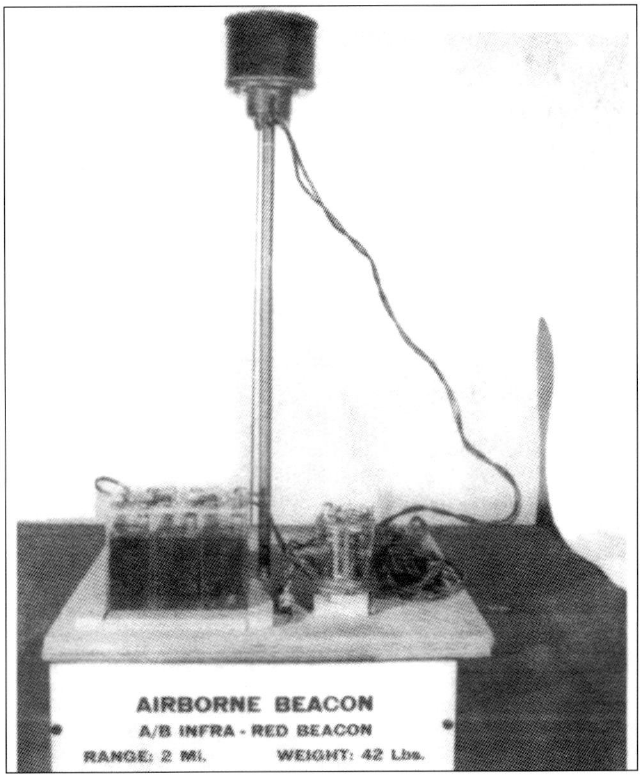

Above: Airborne Beacon. *Courtesy of National Infantry Museum, Ft. Benning, GA* Left: A pathfinder with the Airborne Beacon in use during an exercise. *Courtesy of National Infantry Museum, FT Benning, GA* Below: A display of various pathfinder signaling equipment. *Courtesy of Mark Bando*

Chapter Two

OPERATIONS

SALERNO - September 13-14, 1943

After various plans had been made to jump the 505th Parachute Infantry Regiment, first near the Volturno River, then on Rome, a final mission was received in early September 1943. This mission as planned and executed involved jumping on the night of September 13 and 14 behind the lines of friendly troops, the VI Corps, then engaged to the North and East of Paestrum, Italy.

Fortunately, the Regiment had been on air alert status for a seven day period and all the physical labor that remained to be done prior to take off was to load equipment bundles, which were already packed, and draw personnel chutes. Plane assignments and take off airdromes had been previously designated, however, a time schedule remained to be worked out.

The three planes carrying the fifty Pathfinders from Headquarters Company, 1st Battalion, 505th Parachute Infantry Regiment would depart Agrigento airfield, Sicily at 2100 hours on September 13th for Operation Giant I, followed by the 3rd Battalion, 504th Parachute Infantry Regiment in thirty minutes, and the other companies and battalions at various intervals within the following hour.

The pathfinders were organized one week prior to the combat jump at Agrigento, Sicily. They spent time familiarizing themselves with the equipment: nomenclature, operation and method of wearing them. Their training was conducted by a burley British Sergeant supervised by British officer. Four devices had been developed for the pathfinders; a battery-operated beacon known as the Krypton light, the 5G radio transmitter, and a portable Eureka radar beacon which could send signals to a receiver known as Rebecca in the C-47 transport aircraft (all covered in chapter one). The men actually became proficient at setting up the equipment blindfolded in a few minutes. The pathfinders would jump with two thirty-three pound 5G radar sets and twelve blue Krypton lights.

The electronics in all the aircraft were modified to receive the 5G radio homing signals and sixteen aircraft were equipped with Rebeccas to receive the Eureka radar signals. The lead planes for each group and squadron were the only aircraft equipped with Rebeccas.

A large portion of the personnel had made a previous equipment test in a practice operation at Enfidaville, North Africa (known as "Snowball") on the nights of 28 and 29 August 1943. In this operation the two sets of radar were both ready for operation within five minutes after drop time. However, the test of some of the equipment brought mixed results. The Krypton lights could not be seen because of ground haze and moderate cloud cover. A nearby high-frequency radio transmitter blanked out the signals of the 5G radio beacons. The Eureka-Rebecca system was the greatest success. On the first night of the practice landings, the pathfinder pilots picked up the Eureka signals from fifteen to twenty miles and got them directly over the DZ. The second night parachutist jumped with the sets and were successful in bringing the transports to the DZ.

To avoid a repeat of the faulty Sicily airborne operation, timing and coordination had become paramount planning considerations. For that reason, the Troop Carrier wing and group commanders were at Licata for a briefing on the Naples airborne mission when Ridgeway received the revised plan from Clark. After consultation, another briefing was held to finalize the flight routes to the new DZ. By 1600 the commanders left for their airfields to marshal their units for Operation 'Giant I'. After returning to their 52nd Wing headquarters at Agrigento, General Clark and his operations officer, Lt.Col. Joel Crouch, briefed the three pathfinder aircraft crews and the parachute teams. The three Pathfinder planes were loaded as follows:

First Plane: Piloted by Lt.Col Joel Crouch – Jump Master Col. James Gavin
Lt. Konar, with one radar set to be put into operation immediately.
Lt.Col. Charles Billingslea, with one SCR 536 to notify Plane No. 2 in case of accident.
Cpl. Houston, to assist Lt Konar.
Cpl. Fitzgerald, with team of two men equipped with flashlights to augment DZ markings if necessary.
Two rifle men from 307th Engr Bn. to provide security.

Second Plane: Pilot unknown – Jump Master Maj. Mulcahy with SCR 526 to provide communication with Plane No. 1.
Cpl. Huth, with one radar set to be ready for operation pending mishap to team in Plane No. 1.
Cpl. Girado, to assist Cpl. Huth
Same light and security teams as Plane No. 1.

Third Plane: Piloted by Maj. Brown – Jump Master Capt. John Norton
Capt. Wight
Lt. Cooperider, in charge of light crews
Same light and security teams as Plane No. 1.

Lt.Col. Billingslea accompanied the 504th Para. Inf. on the jump that night, he was previously an observer.
Lt. Cooperider's light crews were to assemble on center of DZ or center of 'T' of lights.

These officers played major rolls in conducting and supporting the 2-3 week test/experimental program. Back row left to right: Capt. John Norton, S-3, 505th PIR, 82nd Airborne Division; Lt. Mike Chester, A Co. 505th PIR; Lt. Bob Bales, 2nd Bn. 505th PIR; unknown, unknown radar technician. Front row left to right: Capt. William Kirkpatrick, Air Corps, Lt. Col. Jno Smiley, S-3, 82nd Div. Arty., Capt. Frank Boyd, 376th Para. F.A. Bn., Lt. Konar, 509th Para. Inf. Bn., unknown. *Courtesy of LTC John Norton*

Pathfinders of the 505th prior to the Salerno jump. Standing left to right: R. Knopf, L. Girardo, J. Ospital. Kneeling left to right: G. Huston, G. Nelson, M. Fitzgerald, J. Huth. *Courtesy of Jerome V. Huth*

Capt William S. Kirkpatrick representing the IX Troop Carrier Command, U.S. Army Air Corps on the right, and Capt. John Norton representing the 82nd Airborne on the left. Photo taken at Comisco, Sicily in October, 1943. *Courtesy of LTC John Norton*

Jerome Huth of the 505th with quick release bag containing transmitter used in Salerno operation. Note: this rare photograph shows both pattern British made leg bags; the early large and later smaller versions. *Courtesy of Jerome V. Huth*

Battalion and separate unit commanders were assembled at 1600 hr., and given the situation and plan to be executed. The DZ chosen was located inside the lines about four miles just north of the Solofront River and about six miles south of the Sele River, near Paestum, in the southern sector of the beachhead. It was on flat land between the highway and the river, approximately 1200 yards long and 800 yards wide. It was to be marked by a 'T' of white lights. The horizontal line was to represent the "Go" line.

Col. William Yarborough stood on the beachhead listening for the three C-47s at 2255 hours. Jerry cans filled with gasoline soaked sand were placed every fifty yards, and a soldier stood next to each container. When Yarborough would hear the C-47s, he would fire a Very pistol and shot a green flare into the dark sky. That would be the signal for each soldier to light his jerry can, and a fiery 'T', each leg a half-mile long would suddenly appear. Some pilots reported seeing the fire from seventeen miles away.

The Pathfinder team departed on schedule at 2100 hours after a brief conference concerning the DZ location and a final review of each man's job. It was evident at the time that the navigation of the lead plane would largely govern the results of the Pathfinder work. They flew in a close 'V' formation at an altitude from 6000-7000 feet along a prescribed course just inside the north coast of Sicily, passed immediately north of Mt. Etna, then northeast of Italy, then north along coastline to point opposite Solo-Frone River, then east to the Drop Zone.

At about 2305, Lt.Col. Crouch's three planes of the 52nd Troop Carrier Wing were approaching from the south. In the open door of the lead plane was Lt. William B. Jones. Behind him were Sgt. Milton Knight, Sgt. Regis J. Pahler, and the rest of the stick. Pahler would bail out lugging the seventy-five pound Eureka radar beacon strapped to his right leg with a quick release attachment, which was to be lowered as soon as his parachute opened. He drew the assignment he had drawn because he was the biggest and strongest man in the group. The others would also parachute carrying parts of the homing devices.

Just as Crouch called out, "The DZ should be right ahead," Brilliant pyro-techniques erupted in the sky and on the ground, a green flare and then a flaming T.

"Let's go!" Lieutenant Jones yelled, and he leaped out, followed in split-second fashion by the stick. Most of the fifty pathfinders in the three planes landed in a tight pattern on the drop zone.

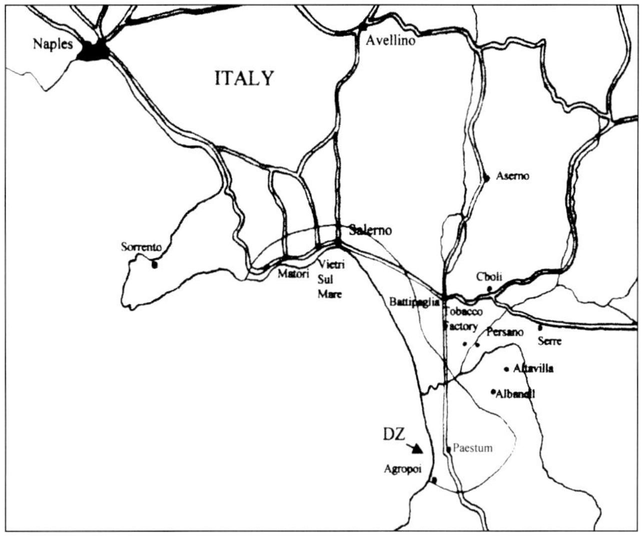

Map of the Salerno Beach area.

Pahler recalls: "Instead of releasing the seventy-five pound Eureka from my right leg, I hit the ground with silk in my hand and the Eureka still attached to my leg. Momentarily, I thought that I had a broken leg, but such was not the case. I set up the Eureka immediately and with Col. Billingslea beside me, we could hear the planes triggering in on the set. Within minutes, the main body of troops began to jump right over the set. What a beautiful site to behold!"

They jumped at 2338 from an altitude of 700-800 feet south of Paestrum, Italy. Upon landing the team quickly assembled and set about putting their gear into operation for the incoming planes. The first group landed squarely on the DZ; the second in a ditch alongside it. They had jumped with 5G radio transmitters, Eureka radar sets, and blue Krypton lights. One of the 5G transmitters broke loose and smashed in the landing; another was held in reserve and never used, since they had little faith in them anyway. In three minutes Lt. Konar's Eureka radar set was in operation. Cpl. Jerry Huth (standing by) had his set ready for operation. The blue Krypton lights were not needed, as the gasoline sand fire signals were operating in good order.

The use of radar equipment was definitely proven as most successful. The marking of the DZ was satisfactory from the standpoint of results achieved and the situation of jumping behind our lines. It is believed, however, that under normal circumstances Krypton Lights or Aldis Lamps would be more practical from the security viewpoints. Smoke Pots as used consisted of gasoline and sand, and threw off a considerable flame.

Plane recognition was accomplished with Amber Lights on the underside of the wings. The lights were easily visible from the ground. Plane formations flew directly over friendly ships in the harbor at Paestum, and also over shore installations. Previous instructions to shore and naval gun crews had been given – not to fire on transport aircraft. These instructions with the additional aids of Amber Recognition Lights were most necessary and no doubt helped prevent a reoccurrence of the disaster, which met the 2nd lift in the Sicilian Operation two months previous. The burning 'T' was extinguished. So far, so good.

At 2325, about fourteen minutes after the first pathfinder had landed, lead C-47s carrying the 2nd Battalion neared the target. The Very pistol was fired and the flaming 'T' was again lit. In moments, the dark sky was filled with scores of white parachutes, coming down towards the center of the drop zone. The remaining units of the 504th landed as scheduled without incident.

On the following night Col. James Gavin's 505th Parachute Infantry Regiment was to parachute onto the same drop zone used by the 504th. 131 C-47s would carry the 2100 plus paratroopers in three serials again by battalions. The 3rd battalion was followed by the 2nd then the 1st.

Again with Lt.Col. Crouch at the controls of the lead C-47, the 505th pathfinders leaped out and landed almost on top of the fiery 'T'. Fifteen minutes later the 3rd Battalion arrived. Less than hour after the last of the 505th landed they were loaded onto trucks and taken to the assembly area.

Pvt. Mathew Kantala of I Co., 504th Parachute Infantry Regiment, 82nd Airborne Division. *Courtesy of Ben Overhand*

AVELLINO - September 13, 1943

With help and knowledge from the British Airborne, company commander Capt. Howland and his executive officer 1st Lt. Fred E. Perry of the 509th parachute Infantry Battalion worked hard to develop usable techniques to get their paratroopers to the correct drop zones. Perry recalls, "Everyone knew through hard experience that the Air Corps needed help to drop us on the correct drop zones. We organized the Scout Company for this purpose. This was later made into a Scout Platoon under my command, consisting of ten enlisted men and myself. We were equipped with a British homing radio and U.S. Navy Aldis lamps, which radiated a beam to guide planes. We trained on this procedure until the invasion of Salerno."

The 509th's Pathfinder detachment was a platoon of the Scout Company. Drop Zone 'A', a large open field three miles east southeast of Avellino was their target. The Pathfinders, nine soldiers led by Lt. Fred Perry and Lt. Henry Rouse, would fly thirty minutes ahead of the main lift and set up the drop zone. Once done, they were to look for the British relief force.

A little after 2145 hours on July 14, 1943, a single C-47 piloted by the commanding officer of the 35th Troop Carrier Squadron, and carrying the eleven pathfinders, took off from Comisco airfield, Sicily for the 325 mile flight to the drop zone. As the lone Scout plane neared Salerno and passed over German lines north of a bridgehead, the plane was rocked by shell explosions, but flew onward. A short time later, Lt. Perry was standing in the door, searching frantically for landmarks on the moonlit landscape. He saw none.

Suddenly a crossroads loomed below, the green light flashed on and out Perry went followed by his team at 2325 hours. They came down unseen and unopposed. Hastily reconnoitering the terrain, they discovered that they had dropped on the wrong crossroads, this one a mile south of the true DZ. There would not be time to march the one mile before the main C-47 serial arrived, so they quickly set up their two Aldis lamps and the 5G transmitter beacon to signal the incoming planes of the 64th Troop Carrier Group. There was no Eureka, because the 51st Troop Carrier Wing had no Rebeccas. The pathfinders settled back to wait for the thirty-nine other planes, bearing the remaining 614 paratroops.

At 2100 hours the remainder of the battalion took off aboard forty planes of the 51st Troop Carrier Wing, 64th Troop Carrier Group. They formed up over the corner of Sicily, flying up the coast of the Italian mainland, keeping well out to sea beyond the range of the shore batteries. During the flight the planes drifted apart, causing some to fly off course. The planes began turning inland and climbing higher to avoid mountains around the DZ.

Around midnight the 509th dropped deep within enemy territory. Lt. Perry later estimated that the first two planes dumped their loads 'directly overhead' of DZ 'A' at Santa Lucia di Sorino. These planes carried Battalion Headquarters personnel with Lt.Col. Yardley first out the door. In the moon's silvery glow the commander walked up to Perry's pathfinders to encourage them, saying "It's working fine. Keep up the good work." Ten planes found the DZ without problems, successfully placing 100 paratroopers. They were from every subunit except Company F. Many of the planes were unable to home in on the pathfinder's light beams. The remainder of the battalion landed widely dispersed. The pathfinder's radio beacon was useless to most for most of the planes due to the mountains deflecting the electronic signals aimed at the approaching planes. The Aldis lamps were nearly impossible for a pilot to pick up unless he was flying a precise course.

NORMANDY: 82nd Airborne - June 6, 1944

Gavin took another interest in the crucial need for developing improved techniques for aiding C-47 convoys to find DZs, especially at night. So in mid-October 1943, Lt.Col. Whitfield Jack, the divisions G-3 (operations officer) announced that a pathfinder experimental team of 125 officers and men was being formed. The team would be returned to Comisco, Sicily to conduct tests. Jack had two pages of questions that General Gavin wanted answered.

T/4 Howard W. Hicks recalled, "Word was sent out to each company for one non-commissioned officers and four privates, to go back to Sicily to join a new team of pathfinders."

Sgt. Rolland J. Duff of the communication platoon of HQ, 2nd Bn, 507th recalls, "While in Portrush, Ireland prior to the Normandy invasion, a call went out for volunteers to train as Pathfinders for the upcoming invasion who would jump prior to the invasion and set up communications, and identify the

Formation of the Scout Company, 509th Para. Inf. Bn.

drop zones for the main echelon of troopers who would be arriving later. I was interested in this and volunteered for this duty."

Capt. Jack Norton a veteran of the Sicily and Salerno jumps, was put in charge of conducting the experiments. Capt. Frank Boyd of the 376th Parachute Field Artillery Battalion flew with the test group from Naples to Comisco.

The 505th, 507th, and 508th Parachute Infantry Regiments each sent six officers and fifty-four enlisted men to North Witham, England for training with the Ninth Troop Carrier Pathfinder Group (Provisional). Personnel from the 82nd Airborne Division formed a Provisional Pathfinder Company. All potential pathfinders were 'hand-picked' from a large group of volunteers. For the Normandy invasion 120 officers and enlisted men would form nine teams, one team for each battalion of the three regiments. Training consisted mainly in practical work – dropping with equipment and organizing drop zones and landing zones for Airborne operations. Special emphasis was placed on night operations.

The only equipment the pathfinder experimenters had were the ninety pound British made Eurekas, which was a back breaking load for a paratrooper to jump with along with his personal combat gear. (Later American versions reduced Eureka's weight to around thirty pounds.) Two 82nd Airborne riggers were brought over from Oran, armed with an ancient sewing machine and a supply of canvas and webbing. Lights for marking glider landing zones at night were made from Delta lanterns.

Riggers Cpl. Danny Bost and Cpl. Robert Shirley promptly put their sewing machine to use and created a canvas pack for the Eureka transmitter that the pathfinders would wear strapped to their leg, and also pouches for the landing lights.

Pvt. Fayette O. Richardson of the 508th Parachute Infantry had joined the Army immediately following the attack on Pearl Harbor. He wanted to be a pilot, but was rejected due to poor eyesight. Instead, he joined the Airborne and shipped to Northern Ireland with the 508th. There he volunteered to become a pathfinder, a decision he did not regret, as his group lived a far more independent and relaxed life than the rifle companies – they were spared KP and guard duties, and were free to come and go pretty much as they pleased after completing their special training in handling the Eureka beacon.

Pvt. John Gerard of the 508th recalled, "I was picked for this duty (pathfinder) because I was a demolitionist and could set booby traps, make explosive charges, etc. All we did was practice our trade and practice some more until we got it right. One week before D-Day our radar man broke his leg so I got the job of radar man along with my regular job as demo man. Going into France I carried thirty-two half-pound blocks of TNT and eight caps and prima cord, a Gammon grenade, and a couple other items. I was so loaded down I couldn't walk so they carried me to the planes and set me by the door."

T/4 Howard Hicks remembers one eventful night during training: "We were enclosed within a high wire fence, having our own kitchen and mess hall. We couldn't talk to anyone outside. We were told D-Day was coming soon and we would be leading the invasion. We got tired of waiting so we jumped the fence and went down the road to a pub. One hour later two MPs came in and ordered us back to camp. We refused to go and soon twenty MPs and two trucks came after us. We decided to go after this. They took us to the jail, but knew they couldn't hold us, so we made all kinds of noise raising hell. They called our CO to get us the hell out of there."

The pathfinder teams consisted of two officers (a Team Leader and an Assistant Team Leader), two Eureka operators, two assistant Eureka operators, Light Section Leader, seven light men, and from four to six security men. The security men were from the 504th Regiment, which would not be participating in the invasion with the division due to the casualties suffered in Italy (they would not be combat ready). Gen. Gavin did ask for 'volunteers' from the regiment for the pathfinder teams and other special missions. Some fifty men stepped forward, twenty-six (two officers and twenty-four enlisted men) of them were dispersed into the teams from the 507th and 508th. The officers went to each regimental team. (The 504th pathfinders would suffer five members killed in action, two missing, and two captured by the enemy. After the invasion in July all the volunteers from the 504th were awarded the Bronze Star for their participation in the invasion.)

As training progressed new ideas and practices were developed. A Standing Operating Procedure was set up to control the training and ensure coordinated action in combat. Instead of the two pathfinder teams per battalion originally envisioned, each battalion group was streamlined to one team. Three pathfinder teams, each representing a battalion of one regiment, were flown to a drop zone in three planes flying in a tight 'V' formation. All pathfinders dropped on the approximate center of a field.

Three weeks prior to the invasion of Normandy the Regimental Pathfinder Leaders from the 505th, 507th, and 508th Parachute Infantry Regiments were ordered to return from North Witham, England to their respective units to be briefed for the coming operation.

The mission of the pathfinder teams was to: organize the drop zones and landing zones; assist battalion commanders in assembling their units; and to deliver to their respective commanders all information of the enemy situation that they had been able to obtain. The 505th Pathfinders were to use green colored halophane lights, the 507th red colored halophane lights, and the 508th to use amber colored lights. Two Eurekas were to be put in operation by each team fifteen minutes prior to their designated time of arrival. The 505th Pathfinder team had the additional mission of setting up the landing zone for the 325th Glider Infantry Regiment.

On June 3, the remaining members of the pathfinder teams were thoroughly briefed on their mission. Aerial photos and maps were examined again and again until the men "knew every blade of grass" on the drop zone and surrounding terrain. The following day the pathfinders were informed of the take off times for Normandy on June 4th. The 505th team was scheduled to take off at 2226 and jump on DZ-O at 0121 on the 5th; the 508th team would leave the field at 2243 and jump on DZ-N at 0138; and the 507th team would follow at 2305 and jump on DZ-T at 0156. However, due to unfavorable weather conditions the operation was postponed twenty-four hours.

The pathfinders of the 82nd sewed small American flags to the upper right sleeve of their jump jackets for identification purposes. They would also would use the password "thunder" with its response "flash", to identify each other in the darkness. Many pathfinders camouflaged their jump suits by painting them various ways with colors of green and black and would also camouflage their faces with burnt cork or soot from stoves for their night jump into France.

PFC Chuck Copping of the 505th said, "Thirty-six hours before the Normandy invasion, a barbed-wire fence went up around the tent city." After they were briefed on where they were going to be landing in Normandy, guards allowed no one to enter or leave or to send or receive mail. To pass the time, movies were brought in. the night before he left for France, Copping, unable to sleep, watched Irving Berlin's newest movie, "Rhapsody in Blue." It was to be a favorite, one he would see many times over the next fifty years.

General Gavin told the pathfinders, "You will have only one friend: God." At all cost they were to avoid trouble. Their vital mission depended on speed and stealth.

Preparations for the 'pay-off' were made in high spirits. The Pathfinders joked, checked equipment, wrote letters, rechecked equipment, posed for pictures, cleaned Tommy guns, sharpened knives, sat and waited, then joked some more. In addition to pathfinder equipment, the men carried field bags and gas masks strapped to their legs, Tommy guns places underneath chest straps, grenades inserted in pouches on their pistol belts, and .45 caliber ammunition and miscellaneous equipment wherever they could cache it. Gammon grenades were carried for use against mechanized vehicles. In spite of the inevitable nervousness prior to the operation, morale could not have been better. The big test, after all of the diligent training of past weeks, was now at hand.

Pvt. Richardson stood in his hut in Nottingham among the rest of the team joking self-consciously with each other as they struggled to stow a mountain of personal equipment about their bodies. A thirty-two pound radar set was strapped below the reserve parachute on his stomach, fragmentation grenades were hooked on his harness, gammon bombs, and a phosphorus grenade, chocolate D-rations, fighting knife, water bottle, anti-tank mine, a morphine syrette, and an armed forces paperback edition of *Oliver Twist* were stowed about his body.

On top of all the kit, he was supposed to carry a rifle. He decided to leave this and make do with a .45 pistol strapped to his high paratroop boot, where he could reach it easily. The pressure of the pistol belt, the tightly laced boots and equipment made him feel oddly secure, as if he were wearing armor. When the trucks came for them, the paratroops tottered forward, floundering like men in diving suits, boosted aboard by the cooks and maintenance men who were being left behind. When the shouted messages of good luck faded away, the men in the back of the truck sat silent, scarcely able to recognize each other beneath the layer of burnt cork on their faces. Then they lay beside the fuselage of an olive drab Dakota in the summer evening silence for almost an hour, drinking coffee and posing for an army photographer. Richardson found himself wanting to stay close to his friends, reluctant to be alone. They were no longer excited, merely tense and thoughtful. Soon after darkness fell, they were airborne.

An hour or so before dark on June 5, all of the 82nd pathfinders teams posed in front of their transport planes and had their pictures taken by the aircrews. After they returned from France many of the men obtained copies of the team pictures.

Their gear was so heavy, some of the men had to be helped into the plane. Copping of the 505th estimates that he may have carried as much as 150 pounds of equipment, including parachute, M-1 rifle, full pack, ammunition and hand grenades.

Because he was in charge of carrying one of the pathfinder's lights to the ground, he also had strapped to his leg a light, tripod and car size battery to power the light. The battery was so heavy, there was concern it might break a paratrooper's leg when he hit the ground.

The pathfinders began taking off from North Witham airfield around 2200 for Operation 'Overlord', the invasion of Europe. They flew in three plane flights, in V-formations at various intervals. The 505th would take the lead, followed by the 508th, then the 507th.

Jammed together in the belly of the plane, they could only talk to their neighbors by yelling over the noise of the aircraft and could only see out of the windows by squirming around inside their great clumsy burdens. Pvt. Lamoureux, alongside Richardson, nudged him and pointed down to the moonlight shining off the water. It seemed to the paratrooper to be frozen in smooth, unmoving ripples. The crew chief clambered down the aircraft to the rear and pulled off the door. Richardson saw a flash of light in the sky outside and understood, after a moment of puzzlement that it was anti-aircraft fire. Then, on the shouted command, they pulled themselves clumsily to their feet and hooked up their static lines to the overhead cable. Now they could see streams of flashing lights coming up from the ground, making harmless popping noise around them, like Roman candles being hosed into the sky. Each soldier felt the pressure of the man behind him leaning into his pack. Then the green light came, and they began the familiar rush to the door in the paratroop one-step shuffle that they had practiced so many times, at last pivoting abruptly before they hurled themselves into the slipstream.

All three teams of the 505th pathfinders hit their correct drop zone 'O', near Ste. Mere-Eglise. Their pilots had mistaken Mounteburg for Ste. Mere Eglise, but caught the error before they jumped. The 505th pathfinder team commanded by 1st Lt. James J. Smith took off as scheduled. His plane piloted by

Air Corps Capt. Kirkpatrick, encountered little flack on the run in from the coast to the DZ. They dropped six minutes early of their designated time and within 400 yards of the previously designated pinpoint.

Pvt. Robert M. Murphy of the 505th fell with a thud twenty yards away and tumbled head over heals into the garden of Madam Levrault as she watch petrified. He recalls, "I took out my trench knife from my boot and cut myself out of the harness. Without knowing it I also cut away pouches carrying three hundred rounds of ammunition." As he grabbed a large bag and stood up the eighteen-year old paratrooper saw Madam Levrault. They stood looking at each other for a long moment and to the old Frenchwoman, the paratrooper looked widely frightening. He was tall and thin, his face was streaked with war paint, accentuating his cheekbones and nose. Then, as the old lady watched in terror, unable to move, the strange apparition put a finger to his lips in a gesture of silence and swiftly disappeared. At that moment, Madam Levrault was galvanized to action. Grabbing up the skirts of her nightwear, she dashed madly for the house. What she had seen was one of the first Americans to land in Normandy. The time was 0015 A.M Tuesday, June 6. D-Day had begun.

Pvt. Murphy lugging his bag with the radar beacon headed out to the garden and started toward his drop zone north of Ste. Mere-Eglise, he heard a short burst of firing off to his right. He was to later learn that his buddy, Pvt. Leonard Devorchak, had been shot at that moment. Devorchak, who had sworn to "win a medal a day just to prove that he can make it," may have been the first American to be killed on D-Day.

All over the area the pathfinders were jumping, some from only three hundred feet. They ran into difficulties from the very beginning. They plunged into chaos. The Dakotas had been swept in over the targets so fast that the Germans at first thought they were fighter planes. Surprised by the suddenness of the attack, flak units opened up blindly, filling the sky with weaving patterns of glowing tracer bullets and deadly bursts of shrapnel.

T/4 Howard Hicks of the 505th recalls, "I was picked to jump with the radar set. It was a big thing, weighing fifty-five pounds. It set on your foot up to your hip with a static line (twenty feet) attached to your harness. Since I had the radar set I was the second to jump. I landed in a field next to a cow, which ignored me. I got out of my chute and assembled with my team."

At 0015 hours, the pathfinders of the 82nd Airborne landed on the drop zones and set up three sets of green lights, one for each battalion, and their Eureka beacon. Fifteen miles away, the main body of aircraft picked up the Eureka signals and at 0204 the first stick jumped.

On his way down, Copping could see red tracers from German guns shooting up at the planes. Because of the intense flak from the ground, many planes were forced off course and discharged pathfinders far off course. Copping was luckier. His unit landed in the exact drop zone, near Ste. Mere-Eglise, a farming community of about 1,500 people.

The first thing Copping heard after landing was a fellow pathfinder by the name of Young whispering his name frantically in the dark. As Young had landed, his rifle dug into the soft soil. Fearing the dirt would plug the barrel when he tried to shoot the gun, Young wanted to borrow Copping's cleaning rod so he could clean the gun before the Germans found them.

The 508th pathfinders were commanded by Capt. Neal L. McRoberts of the 505th and his aircraft was piloted by Air Corps Flight Leader, Capt. Miles. They took off on time, made the French coast on time, and encountered little flak until they reached San Sauveur Le Vicomte. The flak continued until the jumped over DZ 'N'. They landed approximately one and a half miles south and slightly east from the designated DZ. Due to the enemy on the ground only two lights were able to be turned on, one of which in the predesignated code. One Eureka and one Bups beacon was set up and operating twenty minutes prior to the arrival of the first scheduled serial. The Eureka was triggered approximately twelve minutes prior to drop time. The Bups beacon was receiving definite tuning of homing planes. To ground observers it appeared that incoming formations were scattered due to intense anti-aircraft fire. One large formation was observed dropping approximately one mile directly north. Twenty planes dropped on the DZ with the pathfinders ten minutes late of the first scheduled serial. No subsequent serials arrived over the DZ. The Eureka remained on thirty minutes after the time of the last scheduled serial, but no strays dropped during that time.

2nd Lt. Gene Williams and T/5 Frances Lamoureux of the 508th and a few others were the only pathfinders to drop near their designated drop zone 'N' and they were a mile to the southeast of it, near Pont L'Abbe. They did set up their radar beacon and two amber lights, and made contact with the first planes at 0156 hours, when the latter were still twelve miles away, but few pilots picked up the signals.

Pvt. Fayette O. Richardson of the 508th jumped over the fields of the Contentin soon after 0030 hours. He felt a moment of pain on the side of his thighs from his harness as the canopy

Left to Right: General Matthew Ridgway, General James Gavin, Captain Neal Lane McRoberts, and Maxwell Taylor. Captain McRoberts, the commander of all pathfinders in Normandy has just received his second Silver Star for the operation. *Courtesy Deryk Wills*

jerked open, and his head and neck were jerked so sharply that he suffered a brief headache. Then he was floating rapidly down towards an orchard amid a rattle of fire from the ground. He let go the front risers of his parachute, just missing a tree, and slammed into the ground. Ears ringing, he grabbed his pistol and used his spare hand to struggle out of his harness. Then he walked cautiously towards the sound of the little metal crickets that American soldiers were snapping all over the Contentin that night as recognition signals. Through the darkness other men moved to join them. They struggled to free one of the group whose parachute was caught in the top of a tree, and at last cut him down, then they counted heads. Around half the team, including almost all of the men equipped with beacon lights to back up the radar sets, were missing. They had jumped last and landed beyond a road on which the Germans were already audible, driving here and there looking for parachutists. Lamourex, the lead radar operator, switched on his beacon. To Richardson's disgust, having lugged his own set so far with such sweat, he was now obliged to watch the other man pull the internal detonator to destroy it, only one set was necessary. Then they dispersed hastily across the field. The one remaining tripod-mounted light was switched on. The other men pointed their torches towards the sky. Not many minutes had passed before someone shouted, "Here they come!" They saw a new sparkle of anti-aircraft fire, moving closer and closer to them as the planes approached and local guns open up. Then as the first parachutes became dimly visible against the sky, the pathfinders below broke into muted but ecstatic cheers.

After that brief moment of joy when the first wave over the drop zone jumped as planned, they were dismayed to see the second wave approach their signal on the same course, then fly on past the desperately flashing lights without dropping a single man. Only one plane came close to them. Flames were pouring from its starboard engine and the pilot was revving desperately as he lost height, the windows were clearly visible three or four hundred feet above them. A pathfinder sobbed desperately, "Those are our guys." Then the plane disappeared over the horizon and there was silence in the field again. The silence persisted, for the expected third wave of aircraft never came. Instead of a powerful paratroop unit at the assembly point there were only a few dozen men.

Pvt. John Gerard of the 508th, recalled, "We landed where we were suppose to on drop zone 'N' except me, I landed in a tree. Lt. Pollette came and got the radar and my rifle. I injured my arm and it was useless for about three or four weeks. I was later told that I was lucky to be alive."

Cpl. Frank Baumbaugh of the 508th carried the sixty-five pound Eureka and two containers with carrier pigeons. After he set up his Eureka, he was suppose to make a note to that effect and put it in the capsule on the first pigeon's leg and turn it loose. He was told to release the second pigeon at 0630 with info on how things were going, but when he got to the marshaling area he discovered he had no way to feed or water the pigeons, so he let them go. Stripped Brumbaugh weighed 137 pounds, with all his equipment, including his main and reserve chutes he weighed 315 pounds.

Sgt. Elmo Jones of the 505th jumped at 300 feet or so. Just before exiting the C-47 he said a prayer, "Lord, Thy will be done. But if I'm to die please let me die like a man." His chute popped open, he looked up to check the canopy, and just that quick his feet hit the ground. It was a soft landing. His chute settled over his head, "and the first thing I thought without even trying to get out of my parachute was, 'Damn, I just crashed the Atlantic Wall.'"

Jones assembled the team, got seven men with lights in place for their 'T', and told them not to turn on until they could hear the planes. He was one of the few pathfinders in the right place.

The pathfinders of the 507th, were commanded by 1st Lt. John T. Joseph. His plane was piloted by Capt. Minor of the Air Corps. From North Witham they flew to the southern coast of England, across the channel between Guernsey and Alderney Islands, to the west coast of the Cherbourg Peninsula in France. From the coastline it was a straight twenty mile run to the drop zone. The flight over the English Channel was made in close formation without incident. An array of small boats, ships and landing craft spread across the channel as far as the eye could see. It was an impressive and reassuring sight. Some of the men sang, a few slept, most of them chain smoked cigarettes. Off the coast of Normandy "red golf balls" (anti-aircraft fire) rose to harass the "spearhead" of the Airborne invasion. Pilot and pathfinder Leader were in contact through the "Intercom" telephone. After passing the coastline it was decided by mutual agreement to change the jump altitude from 600 feet to 300 feet in order to avoid excessive casualties from small arms fire during the descent. Although no small arms fire could be heard because of the noise of the plane's motors, it was obvious, because of the density of the flak, that the ground was probably as well covered by small arms as the sky was with anti-aircraft fire. The planes dipped to an altitude of 300 feet in order to minimize the effect of the flak. Shortly after the Troop Carriers had flown into the interior of France the parachutists received the red light warning (red signal). They stood up, hooked their static lines to the anchor cable, and checked their equipment for the last time – the drop zone was only four minutes away. Landmarks which had been studied from aerial photos were easily distinguished as the planes made their way inland.

The planes passed the final check point, a dirt road running through the western edge of the drop zone. The pathfinder leader (who doubled as jumpmaster) checked the light signals above the door. As he did so the green light (the "Go" signal) flashed on, and with a shout he disappeared out the door, followed closely by the 3rd Battalion Pathfinder team. The 2nd and 3rd Battalion pathfinders jumped simultaneously. The plane carrying the 1st Battalion team dropped out of the formation approximately two minutes from the drop zone due to the intensity of small arms and 20mm anti-aircraft fire. They were trailing almost a thousand yards to the rear when the 2nd and 3rd Battalion teams received the green light.

The 507th Pathfinders jumped on to DZ 'T' on time just west of Merderet, they were greeted by heavy bursts of machinegun fire and had to fight for their lives from the moment they landed. Two officers broke their legs and several troopers were killed.

1st Lt. Charles Ames dropped accurately on DZ 'T', but could only find his Eureka man, the wire man, and the section sergeant. They encountered rifle and machine pistol fire during the drop but Germans remained in position and did not come after them when they hit the ground several hundred yards from the drop zone. He landed in the middle of a group of buildings, which he recognized at once from prior study of air photos. He backed away from the area at once but came under fire in so doing; moving into a wheat field near the drop zone, he ran into the other men. After waiting vainly for the rest of the team, he sent the men with him on to cover the field and then went on patrol by himself, seeking other members of the team. The search was unavailing and they switched on the Eureka at 0212 hours just in time, for at 0217 the beacon was triggered by a Rebecca response from the leading aircraft of the main body fifteen miles away. At 0226 the main body began to jump filling the sky. Lt. Ames saw the men dropping well beyond him. As he explained it, "What had happened was probably this: in the absence of lights the Eureka signals the location of the field. The blip is on the grid coming up to the field; it goes down the scale during the approach; then it wigged out as the plane goes over the field and starts to rise again at a little distance. This couple of seconds between the pilot's puzzlement over not seeing the lights and his sudden awareness that the blip is rising would account for the plane, on a proper course, dropping their sticks well to eastward." He did not know at this time that he was the only pathfinder on the drop zone. He waited for a few minutes and saw the second serial come over. It acted much as the first had done. The third serial was already scattered because of a heavy cloudbank as it approached him and a number of the planes could be seen far off course. Lt. Ames withdrew his men fifteen minutes after the last serial had passed and blew up the Eureka set. On their way to the eastern end of the drop zone they encountered gunfire. Just before daybreak they contacted members of the 1st Battalion team. 1st Lt. Ralph MacGill, leader of the team, had broken both ankles on the jump and had been taken prisoner.

Lt. Joseph could only find a few of his men, Sgt. James Thore carrying the Eureka beacon, and his Assistant Team leader, 1st Lt. Claude V. Crooks, but no lights. After search the immediate area for more men he decided to set up Sgt. Thore's beacon in the corner of the main center field used for the drop zone.

A paratrooper of the 82nd who has drowned in one of the swamps. *Courtesy Michel De Trez*

Lt. Joseph saw twenty of the eighty-three C-47s carrying the 507th go directly over his head, then go and unload the troopers far from the DZ. Their Eureka had malfunctioned. Joseph and the two pathfinders remained in place for thirty minutes until the German tracer streams zipping past forced them to withdraw. About fifteen minutes after the last planes came over.

Immediately after silencing the Eureka the party of three Pathfinders led by Lt. Joseph proceeded directly to a prearranged rendezvous point at the drop zone where they were to contact the Regimental Commander. When they arrived at this spot they found no sign of any paratroopers. The three decided to remain there until daybreak, and if no one showed up, to proceed to the Regimental Command Post, located 1,500 yards southwest of their position. Sporadic firing continued throughout the night. At times German voices could be heard from adjacent hedgerows. It became quite obvious to the three Pathfinders that to keep the Eureka set, classified as secret equipment, with them would not be wise, and they planned to destroy it at the first opportunity by using the purpose detonator installed inside the set.

At daybreak the men made an attempt to reach the Command post but were stopped by sniper fire from several points. After moving 300 yards to the south they found good cover in a hedgerow and remained there through the day. After dark the Eureka set was blown up and the men made their way southward to the location previously chosen for the Regimental Command post. Again, upon arriving, they found no signs of Airborne troops. They stopped here for the remainder of the night and part of the next morning hoping that someone from the regiment would show up. However, no one came. An examination of the area after daybreak showed no signs of recent occupancy. Fighting could be heard to the northwest, and the three men made their way in that general direction, guiding themselves by the sounds of the firing. At dusk they contacted Capt. Paul F. Smith, Commanding Officer of Company F, who directed them to the Regimental Command Post. The Regimental Commander had assembled approximately 150 men who were holding a defensive position about 500 yards west of Amfreville.

Many of the sticks of the 507th overshot the DZ and landed in the swamps causing many to drown, sometimes in only three feet of water due to their heavy loads of equipment. They dropped between the Merderate River and La Fiere Bridge.

Sgt. Rolland Duff of the 507th recalls, "our group was engaged almost immediately by the opposition, almost being knocked out as an effective team. After suffering these losses seven of our twenty men were able to reach our assembly point. My job was that of the Eureka operator and I was able to set up my machine in an open field with the remaining five men and one officer providing security to protect the machine and me from the enemy."

"I operated my machine until approximately 0145 A.M. until we were certain that all planes able to make it in had arrived. Our regiment dropped within the range of our radar signal with many men dropping in the flooded waters of the Merderet River. I could hear the cries of anguish from my field position along with the enemy gunfire directed spasmodically into my area and that of the men into the waters. Our team was later under commended by the 9th Troop Carrier Command for our successful mission having provided the signal for the plane carrying General Gavin who dropped on line with our position and not over a quarter of a mile away, which I was able to find out later. Lt. Charles Ames was in charge of our group taking over after Lt. Ralph McGill was injured and was captured by the enemy."

"After our mission was completed we started to withdraw from our positions and came under fire again so I detonated the radar equipment to keep it from falling into enemy hands. We joined with a group of men from our regiment and were directed to go to the town of Chef Du Pont where we cleared the town of enemy."

The first Battalion team, led by 1st Lt. George R. O'Brian, landed approximately 500 yards southeast of the drop zone. The use of assembly lights was prohibited by a German machine gun, which was firing in the immediate area. Lt. O'Brian joined the Eureka operator after he hit the ground, and together they moved to the southeast edge of the drop zone and attempted to put the set into operation. The set would not work, however, so after the final serial had passed they blew it up and worked towards the eastern end of the drop zone were the bulk of the parachutists had dropped. On the way they met 1st Lt. Charles Ames and three men from the 2nd Battalion team. Both team members joined the main forces at the eastern of the drop zone. One Eureka set was lost on the 1st Battalion jump. Straps supporting the set snapped with the opening shock of the parachute and it broke away from the operator.

Pvt. Milton Nielson a mortar man from HQ Co., 3rd Bn, 507th jumped with a Eureka beacon onto DZ 'T'. Upon landing he and other members of his team were under German fire before they could remove their chutes. The skirmish proved costly and only a few managed to escape with their lives. What few escaped were hunted relentlessly for six days and nights? During this time the small group did all they could to impair the German war machine. They wiped out gun nest and destroyed personnel positions. They wreaked havoc throughout the German lines and left a trail of death and destruction wherever they went. Overwhelming numbers finally cornered the small group on the night of the sixth day and they were pinned down by machinegun fire. After talking over the situation they decided that the best defense was a good offense and Nielson and Pfc. Jimmie MacCormick went forward into the face of this withering machine gun fire to knock out the position. MacCormick was killed as he was about to rush the nest and Nielson was hit in the legs and crippled. Milton recalls, "A couple of the guys bandaged my thighs and gave me morphine." The first night passed and the rest of the men managed to move out of the area under the cover of darkness. They left believing Nielson and MacCormick dead. "When I woke up it was in the middle of the night so I started crawling to find a better place to lay. I found a drainage ditch and climbed into it. There I stayed for a six days. At the end of the ditch was a small forest of trees, which I crawled to a night. There was a small trickle of green water there. I would soak my hanker chief in it and squeeze the water into my cup. I would do this every night."

"There was a machine gun set up about seventy yards from me. When I'd moved they would see the reeds move and then would come the burst from the machine gun. Finally, I could hear our artillery and dive bombers come over. The bombs threw dirt on me several times but they got ride of the machine gun. The seventh night I started crawling towards our gunfire. Soon somebody called 'Halt'. I was hoping it was Americans and it was. The two soldiers from the 90th Infantry Division helped me walk back to their company. They sent for the Colonel and he came to talk to me. We were standing talking when he said, 'What is that awful smell?' I said it was my leg. He said, 'Get this guy to a medic.'"

Pvt. Nielson was evacuated to the coast to be returned to England. He recovered from his wounds and would jump into Germany in 1945.

Pvt. Thomas H. McCarthy, one of the volunteers from the 504th, jumped from only 300 ft. directly above German soldiers. He landed in a field by a German barracks. After quickly getting out of his parachute harness, he moved into the high grass and waited and watched the Germans. The Germans began to search for him and two of them walked right past him. After letting them pass by, he then threw a grenade and killed them.

The 505th pathfinders sustained only a few casualties due to enemy action. The 507th team reported twenty men missing, killed, or captured and the 508th lost approximately two-thirds (65%) of their enlisted men and officers. Of the twenty-six volunteers of the 504th that jumped with the pathfinders eight were killed in action. All navigational aids used by the pathfinders were recovered and consolidated in the Division Command Post with the exception of those that were destroyed to avoid their falling into enemy hands.

By General Order number 34, Headquarters 82nd Airborne Division, dated 21July, 1944, the 82nd Airborne Division Pathfinders were awarded the Bronze Star medal for gallantry in action on the Cherbourg Peninsula.

NORMANDY: 101st Airborne - June 6, 1944

Maj.Gen. Paul L. Williams, the commander of the Air Corps IX Troup Carrier Command landed back at his headquarters at the airfield near Grantham, England on February 25, 1944. The primary task facing him was to organize a new command and coordinate airborne training exercises with the 82nd and 101st Airborne Divisions for the invasion of France.

The first thing he did was establish the IX Troup Carrier Pathfinder Group (Provisional) with Lt.Col. Crouch the commander and Maj. James T. Blair, Jr. the group's executive officer The group was to provide pathfinder crews and aircraft for airborne missions. It was also to be the command's pathfinder school for crew from the various Troop Carrier groups and paratroop teams from the 82nd and 101st Airborne Divisions. First located at Cottesmore, it was moved to North Witham, ten miles south of Grantham, on March 22, 1944.

In late December 1943, Maj.Gen. William 'Billy' Lee, the father of the airborne program and commander of the 101st Airborne Division called one of his highly regarded young officers, Captain Frank L. Lillyman, and ordered him to train and command a group of pathfinders. They would jump first and direct the main bodies of paratroops to their drop zones and landing zones. "You'll have the total support of my staff and every commander in the 101st," Lee told him. A call went out to the regiments and battalions for 'volunteers' to take part in a highly secret mission. Candidates were to have a background in communications and be able to send and receive Morse code.

Lillyman had problems getting suitable men for his pathfinder group. Gen. Lee cooperated tremendously in developing Lillyman's group. His unit leaders leaped at this opportunity to get rid of their unwanted.

Lillyman recalled, "Many commanders figured that here was an excellent opportunity to get ride of their eight balls by sending them to my pathfinder group. I had no TO (table of organization) so there was no rank among enlisted men. I had inherited former first sergeants and other NCOs, who were excellent men, but who had been busted to private because they had been discipline problems. A few didn't even know what the Morse code was."

It took Lillyman seventy-two hours to screen his first batch of recruits. They then rushed to see Gen. Lee. Lillyman told him that a gang of misfits had been dumped on him. Without a word, Lee turned to his chief of staff, thirty-four year old Gerald Higgins, and said, "Gerry, see to it that this situation comes to a halt." Lillyman sent about seventy-five percent of his recruits back to their units, much to the dismay of their commanders who hadn't expected them to return.

Cpt. Frank Lillyman in 1945 when he commanded the 101st MP Co. *Courtesy of Mark Bando*

Again the call went out for 'volunteers', and the pathfinder ranks were once again filled. Charles R. Malley, from F Company of the 506th Parachute Infantry Regiment, a "busted" private who was Lillyman's acting first sergeant, remembered his pathfinder protégés: "We had a bunch of good guys who had screwed up one way or another. Our pathfinder unit was stationed just outside Nottingham, home of Robin Hood, and the famous bastille where good ole' Robin had been incarcerated. Many were the times that I received calls from the sheriff of Nottingham to come get our present day hoods out of jail. The good thing about English justice – no fines, no nothing – just get them the hell out of here."

Malley continues, "When I returned from Robin Hood's jail with the bodies, Capt. Lillyman made inquiries as to the seriousness of the offenses or any damages inflicted on the English citizenry. If the situation seemed bad, he gave the guy company punishment, forestalling a possible court martial. He saved me once that way."

As the first men to land in enemy occupied France, the pathfinders were viewed as a potential "suicide squad," and in the years since the war, a definite mystique has attached itself to the men who served in that capacity. It is interesting to see how the actual selection was done.

T/5 Joseph Haller's company commander requested that he volunteer. "We'd like to have you in the Pathfinders because you can speak German," Capt. Simmons told him.

"If it's my time to die, I'm going to die no matter where I am," Haller said. "If you want me in the Pathfinders, I'll join the Pathfinders." There was more to it, however. Haller often talked pro-German around his buddies to entertain himself and to provoke them. "Today Germany – Tomorrow the World, then I shall rule in this district!" Haller would loudly proclaim.

Joe's best buddies were Joe Dejanovich, a Siberian trooper, and David Hadley. "The Three Kings," Haller called them. All were from the communications platoon and worked together as a team through training. But Capt. Simmons suspected that Dejanovich was a Communist – he had been heard threatening to go over the hill once he landed on the continent so he could join Tito and fight with the partisans.

Lt. Albert Watson, known as "The Gremlin," was the battalion mess officer and not popular with the top officers in 1/501. Somehow, he wound up volunteering for the Pathfinders, along with "The Three Kings."

Many members of the division were never given the opportunity to volunteer for pathfinder duty as the slots were filled before they even heard about the outfit.

Around February 1944, Leonard Newcomb of F/501 was in his tent at Hamstead Marshall, minding his own business, when Lt. Hugh Hendrickson, the executive officer of his company, walked in and stated that volunteers were needed for a special outfit to jump in ahead of everyone else in the invasion to signal the other planes. In a letter to Mark Bando dated April 16, 1973, Newcomb wrote: "I asked him if he was going in it and he said yes – so Joe Bass and I both said okay. Red Larsen who had the first bed in the tent said he wanted to be in it, so Lt. Hendrickson said yes. Harold Sellers came in the tent to get mail at this time, and said he wanted to join – for we were all in the same squad."

Thus were all the available slots for F/501 filled only one other slot was available and Ralph "Pinky" Newton of F/501's 2nd Platoon got it. No one from 3rd Platoon even had a chance to volunteer before the slots were filled. Also, Leo Gillis of the company points out, certain noncoms of a company wouldn't have been allowed to go, either.

The 2/501 group of volunteers had little idea at the time that they would land on Drop Zone 'D', the hottest of all on D-Day. Sellers was killed upon landing, becoming the first F/501 in the war. Newcomb was captured on D-Day afternoon and spent the duration as a prisoner of war.

At this point, there is a necessity for elaborating on the makeup of this group. Much of the material herein was secret until many years after the war. A total of eleven sticks of jumpers were trained by the 101st Airborne Division for the D-Day mission. A team of three sticks was assigned to each of the three parachute drop zones while two sticks were to prepare the way to the glider landing fields. Each stick was composed of from eight to twelve pathfinders. Shortly before D-Day a security detail was assigned to each stick by the Division. They were to cover the pathfinders on the drop zones while these men concentrated on directing the incoming planes.

On February 25, 1944, Maj.Gen. Paul Williams and his staff rushed up from the Mediterranean to take over the IX Troop Carrier Command. Williams seemed to be the ideal choice, he had gained wide experience directing troop carrier operations in Sicily and Italy and he was tuned to the same wavelength as the often temperamental airborne leaders.

Gen. Williams command consisted of Hal Clark's veteran 52nd Troop Carrier Wing from the Mediterranean, and two wings fresh from the states, the 50th and 53rd wings would tow the gliders.

With Williams's carrier command now open for business, a pathfinder school was established at a brand new airfield, North Witham, near Grantham, England. It was a hundred miles to the north of the 101st Airborne Division Headquarters. Col. Joel Crouch, the pathfinder pioneer who had flown the lead C-47 plane for previous drops, had come up from the Mediterranean and was put in command of the North Grantham School. His executive officer was Lt.Col. James T. Blair. Pathfinder candidates from both the 82nd and 101st Airborne Divisions would learn their techniques here.

More than 350 American and British personnel trained at the school prior to the Normandy invasion. There was no TO&E or precedent for the training. The password at North Witham was 'teamwork'. Each pathfinder team consisted of nine to fourteen signaling specialist with two Eureka sets and nine Holophane lights, plus a five-man security detachment to protect them while they performed their signaling functions. Each team of pathfinders were assigned a particular C-47 and a specific crew. They worked, ate, and lived together as a team. Col. Crouch and his officer staff lived at one end of the barracks, while the paratroop officers lived at the other end.

All pathfinder officers, both C-47 pilots and paratroops, were put through an orientation course so that each could

Volunteers of the 2nd Bn., 501st Para. Inf. Regt. At Newbury, England, before going to Pathfinder school at Nottingham. Standing Left to Right: Pfc. Harold E. Sellers (F),?,Pfc. Robert E. Sechrist (E), Pfc. Robert A. Howarth (D), ? . Kneeling: unknown, Laying down: Sgt. Joe Bass (F) (KIA Korea), Pvt. Ralph A. Newton (F) (KIA Bastogne). *Courtesy of Mark Bando*

101st Airborne Pathfinders of the 501st take a break from training at Nottingham. *Courtesy of Mark Bando*

A pathfinder team being inspected by Winston Churchill. Signal panels, Holophane lights, and an antenna for a Eureka beacon are visible on the left. *Courtesy of the National Archives*

understand the problems of the other. Paratroop enlisted and officers learned how to start and taxi a C-47, and the principles of aerial navigation. Some of the more gung ho air crew officers were given a crash course and became qualified parachutist.

For better accuracy, the aircraft's navigators needed only to apply conventional calculations to verify the distance and time from the objective. From experience in training exercises, the Rebecca was restricted to use by flight leaders in each normal nine-plane formation. Too many aircraft using their Rebecca receivers, possible in a large formation, could overload the Eureka transmitters. The result was distorted and inaccurate information. The radar technicians assigned to the pathfinder groups imposed other restrictions, such as the specific channels chosen for the Eureka transmission and when during the flight the Rebeccas should be operated.

Student pathfinders jumped five to seven times each week, with at least two at night, because they would be dropped at night in Normandy. They were put on special high calorie diets to enhance night vision. The pathfinders were learning the use of radar, lights, smoke, luminous panels, and how to use the Rebecca-Eureka navigation systems. They also learned how to set up the special Holophfane lights, use the British Gee navigation system, the SCR-717 radar, and to use the BUPS beacon.

On the night of May 11, during the great rehearsal, Exercise Eagle, for the Normandy invasion, seven pathfinder teams of the 101st Airborne led off. All did well in finding the assigned DZs and getting equipment into operation except one, which became lost in a haze, and did not reach the DZ in time to be of any assistance. Half an hour later, over 6,000 paratroopers of the 101st Airborne followed in 432 aircraft. The exercise went very well and those who planned the drop hoped the real invasion would go just as well.

Crouch's pilots, navigators, and crews were honing their abilities to navigate at night and to locate a certain point with a particular Eureka-Rebecca set.

Each stick was led by an officer who jumped with his combat load of equipment, and an SCR-536 radio to be used in communicating with other officers of the three sticks who jumped as part of the team, on the same drop zone.

Two men in each stick jumped with Eureka radar sets. These devices sent out continuous signals, which were to be received by the leading aircraft in each serial of planes. The reception was through a companion set known as Rebecca. Immediately upon landing, these sets were made operational. Quickly preparing them for operation was important to the pilots

Capt. Lillyman briefs some of his men from a sand table during training at North Witham. *Courtesy of Michel De Trez*

Capt. Lillyman talking with one of the C-47 air crews before a training jump. *Courtesy of Michel De Trez*

Capt. Lillyman departs for a training jump before the invasion. *Courtesy of Michel De Trez*

who could then begin receiving signals that the "trail blazers" had landed.

Four men carried lights of the Holophane type in canvas bags under the reserve parachute. Each of the four men jumped with two lights. Seven of the lights were used in a 'T' arrangement. The tail of the 'T' pointed in the direction of the jump; the crossbar of the 'T' indicated the "go" point. These lights were set into a position where they were easily visible from the air, but almost completely hidden from ground observers. When the motors of the approaching aircraft were heard, the lights were illuminated. The taillight (tail of the 'T') was coded to blink out the signal of the drop zone. (Example: On Drop Zone 'A' the light blinked out – Morse code signal for the letter A). These lights were also coded in color per drop zone. (Drop Zone 'A' was amber; 'T' was green; and 'D' was red.)

The operator of the lights had a battery with a telegraph key, which was on a twenty-five foot extension cord. The key operator remained at his post throughout the operation, while the remaining men served as security personnel to protect the equipment. The Eureka performed independently when set in operation and was sometimes placed in a tree.

For daytime operations, the men also carried panels and smoke grenades to be used in conjunction with the Eureka sets.

Capt. Lillyman had a general briefing concerning the invasion as early as the middle of May. He commented: "I knew the general time and place of deployment of our people. Likewise, I had been briefed on the British plan and realized that each of us was to go in via parallel routes."

"Of considerable concern to me was the magnitude of the security problem. Until now, briefings had been given to only regimental commanders and key staff officers. I was obliged, in order to assure proper training, to give limited details of the briefings to my officers. After briefing them, I had the constant worry as to whether " security" would be violated."

"This was exemplified by a situation at North Witham when one of my lieutenants, Hendrickson, a commander of one of the sticks, visited blacked out Nottingham. Although our people normally traveled in pairs, he was alone, separated from his partner, and struck by a laundry truck while crossing the street. He sustained, along with other injuries, a fractured leg and was taken to a military hospital. His strong sense of security made him refuse medical attention until I was notified. I was able to send a man to stay with him, to be certain that he did not divulge information while under anesthetic and during recuperation."

The pathfinders didn't move to another area for their staging. When it was time to seal them off, security personnel

Fully loaded 101st pathfinders prepare to board their C-47 for a training jump.
Courtesy of Michel De Trez

101st Pathfinders depart for a training jump with full gear prior to the invasion.
Courtesy of Michel De Trez

closed off their area with barbed wire. First Sergeant Malley described it: "I think it was in late May that each of the pathfinders realized that we were nearing the day of the invasion. In the last week of May, they threw the 'barbed wire' on us."

"We had gone to a briefing session in another area and when we came back to our own barracks they had a fence put up and MP's were already walking guard," recalled PFC John R. Sample.

This brought several problems in security. Capt. Lillyman recalled, "Another unforeseen problem occurred on the 4th of June. We were marshalling at North Witham Air Base, which constituted, on one side of the field, the Air Force supply depot on which we relied for our administrative support, pay, supplies, etc. Division had increased our mission in having us to take in mines and demolitions. I had put in a requisition for the mines to be delivered at the gate of our barbed-wire enclosure on the fourth of June."

"I was in the orderly room paying my men in French money late on the afternoon of the 4th. Despite our scrutiny precautions, a sergeant came in from the opposite side of the Air Base with these mines and said that the he had orders to deliver them to Capt. Lillyman. He walked past the sentry and into the orderly room where I was paying my men in invasion currency. I immediately realized that this was a compromise and, although he was their chief non-commissioned officer, I had to lock him up. He stayed in that capacity until the 7th of June. Obviously, his section chief on the other side of the airfield was very concerned by his absence. I could not tell him nor would the Base S-2 give him information or to the reason as to why he was locked up. He was concerned by the fact that someone had kidnapped his sergeant and this created a rather embarrassing situation."

Scheduled to parachute with the pathfinders were other personnel, among them, the security forces of the pathfinder group. These men reported into the area around June 1st. Included, also, was a three-man intelligence team, which was to find suitable routes to the beach.

A security soldier for the 501st Regiment, Pvt. John D. Mischler from B Co., recalled, "For a period of time before D-Day we were under 'live-ammunition' guard. We studied maps, overlays, scale models, and information peculiar to the pathfinder mission. Many field officers did not receive this extensive preparation."

Lt. Robert S. Dickson, III, an intelligence officer from the 502nd Regiment, was given a special assignment by his regimental commander. He was to jump with two of his men, with the first planeload of pathfinders: "We were to reconnoiter a route to the regimental objective which was that of the coastal artillery guns, just behind Utah Beach. We spent considerable time studying the road networks to be used in approaching the objective."

Capt. Lillyman described the postponement of D-Day: "on the fourth of June, we had our first 'dry run', which was very touchy. The pathfinders, as usual, were the last ones to get the word. After the evening meal, we returned to barracks, drew all of our equipment, camouflaged our men with face coloring, loaded the aircraft, then sat there and waited, and waited, and waited. Finally cancellation of the mission came through and re again returned to our barracks. We had been scheduled to take off at 2145 in the evening. Meanwhile, many base administrative individuals had driven by the flight line and had seen us in obvious battle uniforms. Of course, they knew that the pathfinders were about to take off."

First Sgt Malley described the delay: "On June 4, a plane came wheeling into the Air Base, and a warrant officer was admitted to the compound. A small valise was attached to the officer's right wrist. Capt. Lillyman's face became quite pale.

A three photo sequence of Pathfinders on a training jump before the invasion. The first two men are carrying the Eureka beacon. *Courtesy of Michel De Trez*

Lillyman read General Taylor's message, which was inside the container. He turned to me, saying, 'Sergeant, tell the troops to relax – we have one more day.' The letter was burned there on the spot. The valise was returned to the warrant officer who had no realization of its contents. The officer departed."

"I remember the cancellation of the jump on the evening of June 4th," said Pvt. John Zamankos. "We had waited on the airport apron for more than two hours, 'shooting the breeze' about days at home. One of the boys had received a 'Dear John' letter. The postponement seemed to have taken the starch out of us."

A warrant officer returned the next day. Malley said, "On the following day at approximately 1800 hours, a new plane, a different officer, but the exact procedure was followed. Lillyman went through the same motions, however, at this time, he turned to me and said, 'Get the troops ready.' The entire company was moved to the flight line, and low and behold, they had photographers, generals, and all-even Red Cross girls with coffee to cheer us." The well known photographs of both the 82nd and 101st Airborne Pathfinder teams were originally taken by Air Corps personnel on the 5th of June and many of the pathfinders upon their return to England obtained copies of their teams picture. Of the twenty sticks of pathfinders all having had their team pictures taken some of the team photographs are missing.

As the brass watched from the apron, the planes moved off to the runway, tested their engines and took off. Malley said, "They issued our 'puke pills' and vomit bags, then 'fired up' the motors. My remembrance is that the hour was near 2200, English time. Due to the fact that I was jumping a Eureka radar set, attached to my right leg, I was the number one man in the door. Naturally we were loaded to the gills with equipment and were barely able to move. We flew over the English Channel, and low enough that the spray, from water, came through the doorway. Later this was said to have contributed to the confusion of the German radar."

PFC John Sample noted that the planes flew a salute over the people gathered below: "We took off and buzzed the airfield, then we went up to around three thousand feet until we left England."

The planes then dropped to almost wave-top level. "There are two things that I remember about the trip," said Sample. "One is that somewhere over the Channel I saw a red flashing light and was told that it was a rescue ship, just in case. The other was that at one time we were so low that the prop blast was blowing water in the door."

The men were to be in Normandy from a half hour to an hour before the main body of troops began arriving.

Lt. Dickson, from his position in the first plane where Capt. Frank Lillyman was jumpmaster, recalled, "I looked out and saw the moon, and the searchlights of the Jersey and Guernsey Islands, blinking the warning of our coming, as we flew by them. I remember the cloud cover over France, and finally, the apparent quiet of everything."

As the planes crossed the coastline and headed inland, from the west side on the peninsula, the unexpected cloud cover caused dispersion, this before the planes were to separate and head for their respective drop zones. Lillyman's three-plane team headed for the northernmost Drop Zone 'A', in the area between Ste. Mere-Eglise and St. Martin de Vareville. This drop zone was assigned to a combat team composed of the 502nd Parachute Infantry Regiment and the 377th Parachute Field Artillery Battalion.

The three planes experienced little or no flak in the trans-peninsula flight. Because of the low clouds and dog at the western side of the Contentin Peninsula, the plane crews failed to pick out the early identification marks. Because of this, the green light was flashed on the approach to the small town of Ste. Germain de Varreville, which was located one and a half miles north of the spot for which the men had aimed.

Capt. Lillyman was suffering intensely and had been for three days. In order not to miss the invasion, he had concealed the fact that he had badly torn leg ligaments in a jump four days earlier, an injury that can take weeks to heal.

Standing in the open door and shivering from the chilly blasts of air, Lillyman could see every detail on the ground in the bright moonlight. Up in the cockpit Cpt. William Culp, the radar operator, notified Col. Crouch and his co-pilot, Capt. Vito Pedone, that the plane was approaching the village of Ste. Germain de Varreville. Moments later the green light flashed on and out the door went Lillyman, with a cigar clenched in his teeth. The No.2 man, Lt. Samuel McCarter and the remainder of the stick. In the C-47, Culp and Pedone recorded the time, 0015, June 6, 1944. They jumped from only 450 feet.

There is some question about if Lillyman was actually the first man to jump from the plane. PFC John G. McFarlan claims a last minute delay in the plane had caused the jumping order of the stick to change slightly, and although Lillyman claimed credit for being the first American to land in France after midnight on D-Day, he was actually the second or third. The two had switched places and McFarlan actually left the plane first. As he points out: "Unless Capt. Lillyman found a way to

101st Airborne Pathfinders of the 501st at North Witham Airfield prior to boarding for the drop. Pvt. Leonard J. Newcomb a pathfinder of F Co. 501st was captured on D-Day is in the lower right photo. *Courtesy of Mark Bando*

beat me to the ground, I was the first to land." He landed near Ste. Germain de Varreville.

Capt. Lillyman pulled hard on his forward risers, and slipped into a small field near the town. He crashed down hard on his already painfully aching leg. Over in the far corner of the field the tall poplars were swaying and casting eerie shadows, and in the shadows, he could tell something was moving. Lillyman loaded his Thompson submachine gun. He slowly moved toward the moving figures and challenged them with his cricket. There was no reply. He was about to fire at them when he heard loud moos. He had landed in a field with cows, Lillyman laughed and moved on. He quickly rounded up seven men who landed nearby. They did a map reconnaissance and realized they were north of their DZ, but because of the lack of time before the main assault force arrived, they decided it was close enough.

Nearby could be seen the contours of a church, and the pathfinders headed toward it. Lillyman decided to set up his Eureka in the steeple. "T/5s Walton and Council shinnied up a tree and set up a Eureka for our sticks of jumpers. Our orders were to do no shooting and we had instructed our men to take evasive action if Germans were sighted," recalled Lillyman.

"A German machine gunner, spotted us through the bushes, kept probing with small burst. This was annoying, and finally I sent two men to convince the Krauts of the 'error of their ways.' Soon I heard a grenade go off with a 'whumf', and then everything was lovely and quiet."

Lillyman continued, "Forty-seven minutes later the planes arrived with the main body of troops. This was the longest forty-seven minutes of my life. Those lights never looked so bright in training, but that night they looked like searchlights. One light went out, and we had to rig an emergency connection. We were silhouetted against it for a few minutes, however, nothing happened."

"Several of my scouts reported a farmhouse, where there were Germans, at the edge of the field. Two others, and myself went to the house where we met a Frenchman smoking a pipe. He was standing in the doorway. He jerked his thumb toward the stairs and said, 'Boche'. We caught the German, in a nice pair of pajamas, in bed. We disposed of him and expropriated the bottle of champagne by the bed."

"We met no more Germans before the main invasion body landed, however, one enemy bicycle patrol approached and then turned back. They seemed to not want any part of us and we wanted no part of them. The rest of Lillyman's stick was strung out over several hundred yards."

These three men were the only members of the 326th Airborne Engineer Battalion, 101st Airborne Division to serve as Pathfinders in Normandy. They were all from C/326th. Left to right: Pfc. Louis DiGaetano (KIA Bastogne), Pvt. Albert Kouba, and Cpl. Calvin Jackson. *Courtesy of Albert Kouba via Mark Bando*

Pvt. John Zamankus observed, "Our flight over enemy territory was a complete surprise to them. The jump was good but I landed alone on the far side of a hedgerow. The radar I had hooked under my chest pack interfered with my straps. In freeing myself from my chute, I had to cut my risers."

"I jumped into a ditch, waited, and listened; then clicking my cricket, crept back along the line of flight. I found other members of my stick – Walton, Jones, and Council. I was radar operator. We brought a few planes into the area and on our field, it was a mess. We had no idea where we were. When the planes did come in, they came in from all points of the compass. We had men of the 505th Regiment of the 82nd Airborne Division jump on our lighted 'T'."

"On occasion, I have wondered about what the Jerries thought. It was so messed up, that no General, of any Army, could have evaluated any part of it. Perhaps that is the reason it was so successful."

Pvt. Raymond 'Snuffy' Smith, a medic was to be the first casualty of the group. He recalled, "The jump was smooth. We jumped near a church at Ste. Germain de Vereville. I landed in an apple tree, in the church yard, and injured a foot on striking the ground."

"Two or three of my group landed within fifty feet of one another. We crawled around the area, snapping our warning bugs. Members of our group assembled, moved off, and set up battery operated lights and radar as jump identification signals for the main body of troops; this providing the fields were clear of enemy and obstacles."

PFC Delbert Jones, jumping from the same plane, remembered, "We had good moonlight and clear weather. The jump itself was very good. I landed in a courtyard surrounded by a stone wall. As I landed, my helmet scraped against the wall, and made a great deal of noise. Because of all the gear I carried, I had difficulty in getting off my equipment. I was very nervous as I lay on my back. I could see a light shining under the door of the house. My thought was, that this was one of those German barracks at the end of our drop zone."

"On freeing my rifle and signal lights from my harness, I attempted to find my way out of the courtyard. Finally, I climbed over the wall and fell into a cemetery among the tombstones on the other side. I recall meeting Gus Mangoni and two other men, one of whom had a fractured ankle. I carried him with us most of the night."

Jones added, "I was a signal-light man and had to set up the pattern 'T' for the arrival of the 502nd and their drop. We only partially completed that part of the task. Finally, I was with Captain Lillyman and a number of others. We proceeded to the coastal gun emplacement, but found that it had been destroyed by the Air Force."

PFC Fred Wilhelm had a difficult time reaching his straps with all the equipment slung from them. He said, "I found after landing I could not reach my chest straps and had a time getting out of my harness. Once free, I put my M-1 together and got my landing lights ready. In about ten minutes, I made contact with T/5 Tom Walton."

"Our mission was to use radar and lights to bring in the rest of the Airborne. We were to form a 'T'. At a given time we were to turn our lights on; the ships were to come up the leg of the 'T' and then give the green light to the men at thee crossbar. After getting into position, I accidentally turned the switch and the light came on. We heard firing and some shell coming after my light came on. I thought we had had it. Then as we had some time to wait, Captain Lillyman and I took a walk down to a farmhouse in which we found a German officer."

"This was quite a drop," said Private Francis A. Rocca, from the same stick. "I landed in the enclosed yard of a parsonage. I collected my gear, then attempted an immediate rendezvous with the others of the stick. We managed to assemble all of our men."

Another plane carrying a second stick from Lillyman's team dropped a short distance away. PFC William H. 'Buzz' Barton, of Dog Battery of the 377th Parachute Field Artillery Battalion remembered, "The night was beautiful and we had some moonlight – no flak. We came in very low. I believe we jumped at 400 feet. We were seen by no one. I landed "smack" in the middle of Drop Zane 'A'."

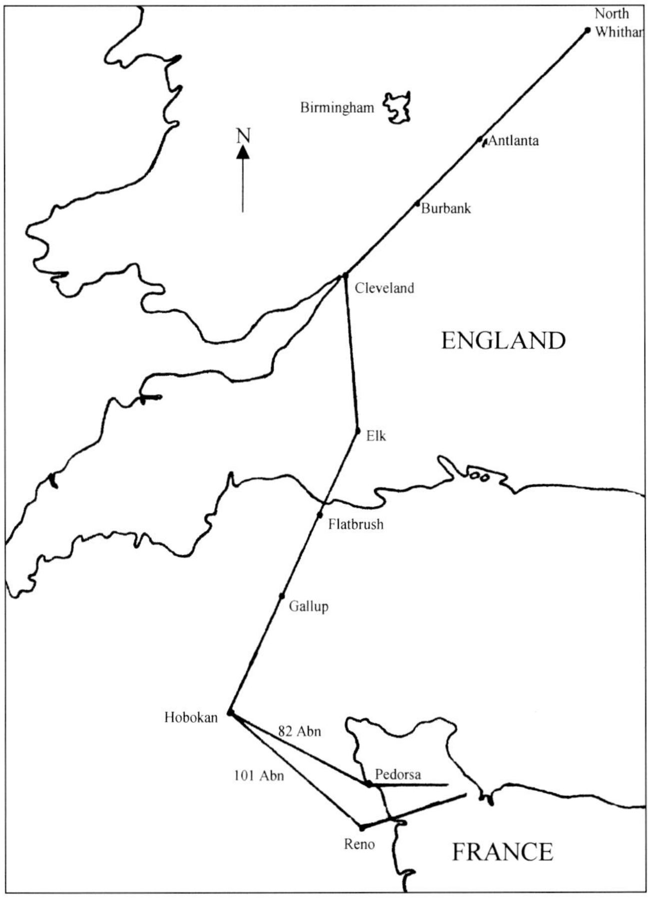

Flight pattern for the 82nd and 101st from North Witham to Normandy.

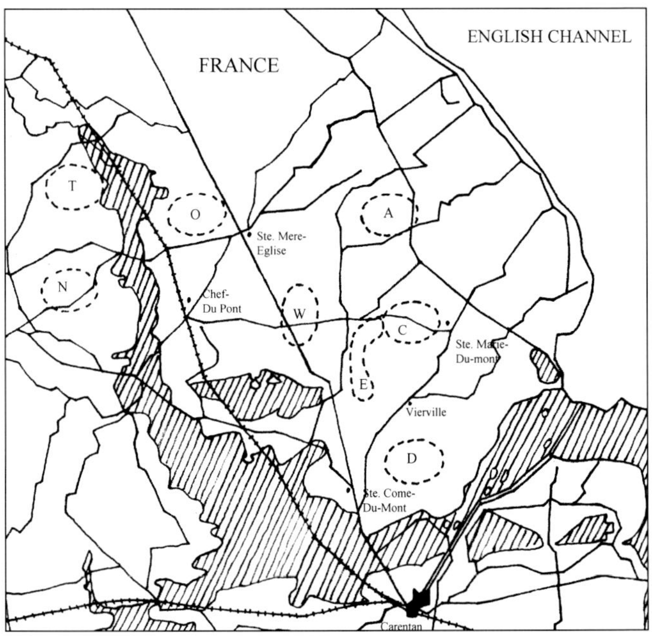

Map of Normandy and the drop zones of the 82nd and 101st Airborne Divisions. The shaded areas are the fields the Germans flooded.

"After getting out of my harness, I contacted the men from our stick. I met Lt. Robert G. Smith and prepared to light the drop zone. I recall that he collected all the men from our stick – we didn't lose a man. My particular assignment was to stand near an amber-colored battery operated light to make certain that it wasn't shot out near the end of the 'T'."

"Having accomplished my particular task, the 'T' was lit up like a Christmas tree, but the troopers jumped every damned place except on the drop zone. After the drop, we moved to an area nearby where we dug in and waited for daylight."

Another member of the stick was PFC John R. Sample who was near the front of the stick had an opportunity to observe some of the action outside the plane. He said, "In our briefings we had been told that the British would be bombing on the coast as we were dropping. I was number '3' man in the door and as we were hooked up and standing ready to go for the entire trip across the peninsula, I saw several sticks of bombs go off as they hit."

"Colonel Crouch flew the lead plane and he told us earlier that they would slow down so we would have a good jump regardless of the situation on the ground and boy, they did just that. It was the best exit I ever had. After my chute opened I saw two objects running across the far end of the field so I frantically climbed my risers and when I got closer to the ground I realized they were cows. What a relief! There was an anti-aircraft gun nearby but with the woods separating us from it we drew no fire-not even small arms."

"We assembled under a big tree that was on the drop zone and then set up our lights radar. We waited several minutes before we turned them on. I don't recall all the parachutists who jumped on our signals but I know that not one plane from our battalion did. I do remember that the first wave of planes off to the right of the 'T' and the lead plane and those with him corrected their line of flight to come right over us. All of our pathfinders were accounted for outside of two or three injuries and they were of minor nature."

In the eighteen man stick, with Lillyman, the last three jumpers were Lieutenant Robert 'Buck' Dickson and his two men from the Regimental S-2 Section. Their departure from the aircraft was different from the previous parachutists. Dickson stated, "My two men and myself were the last to drop. One heavily burdened trooper fell in the doorway just prior to our jumping. By the time we pushed him out, the pilot was diving and turning homeward. This caused our jump to be at a low altitude and a considerable distance from the others.

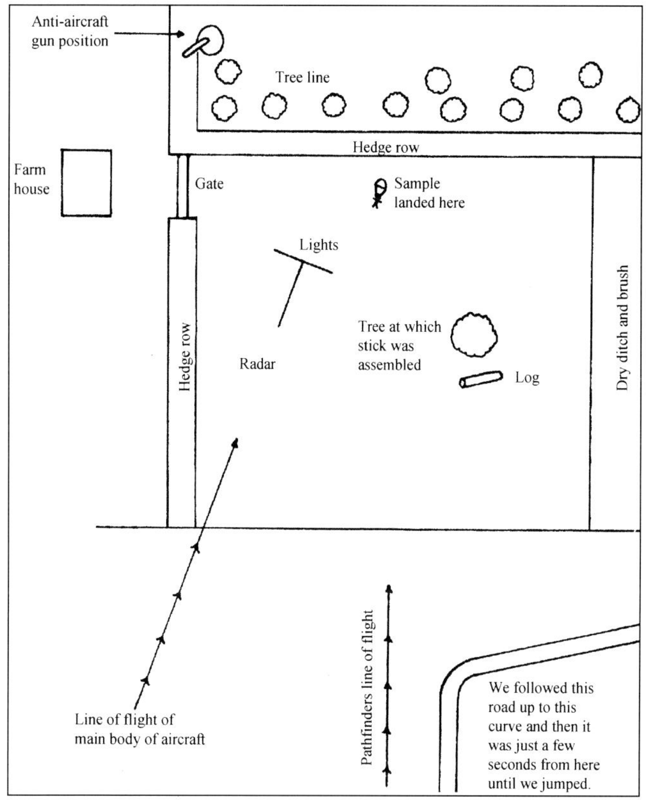

This is a sketch of the pathfinder set-up as remembered by Pfc. John Sample of the 377th Pathfinder stick which landed in the vicinity of St. Germain-de-Varreville on June 6 at approximately 0015 A.M. *Courtesy of George Koskimaki*

"I had no difficulty getting out of my chute except for the nervousness generated by the situation. I set my 'grease gun' (.45 automatic) in tall grass, and then walked away without it. I did some scurrying around and found it. I located my men in the next field; however, we were unable to completely orient ourselves and joined with other small groups from many units, including the 82nd. During our wandering in the early morning hours, a few of us became separated and were fired on from approximately three hundred yards. My 'grease gun' was so ineffective at that distance, I had to cease firing. Later, I picked up an M-1 from a dead soldier – and still later, acquired a carbine, which I considered the best compromise among the three. We did not reach our objective on D-Day."

Between 0200 and 0300, after the main body of troopers had landed, Lillyman and scouting party of twelve men moved out toward the Coast. They discovered that the coastal artillery battery had been demolished.

A second team of pathfinders under the leadership of Lt. Gordon O. Rothwell headed for Drop Zone 'C' near Hiesville. Rothwell's plane was in the lead of the three-plane group. First

Sergeant Malley, a member of Rothwell's stick, described their unusual landing: "Suddenly we shot up a couple hundred feet. The damned flak was all over the sky and tracer bullets were a dime a thousand. Bullets were whizzing through the fuselage like bees chasing a 'honey-robbin' bear. All of a sudden the warning bell to clear the airplane rang out. Normally, being airborne, you go out thinking. I was looking out of the door ready to swing. We were all hooked up and I could have grabbed a handful of trees. I hollered to Lieutenant Rothwell, my stick commander, to hold. One motor was on fire and burning fiercely. The crew chief kept hollering, 'Clear the ship! Clear the ship!'

"Clear the ship hell! We were at ground level. The co-pilot came rushing back into the troop section, and shouting, 'Every thing overboard! We're going down.'

"We cut and slashed our way out of parachutes, guns, ammo, every damned thing we could. I pulled the detonator on the radar set and threw it out. Hell, we had nothing on but jump boots and O.D. uniforms. The co-pilot came back to the cabin again, and made the overstatement of the century. He hollered, 'Prepare to jump. We are going in!"

"Jump hell!"

"I can sincerely state, that there was no great excitement on the plane. I cut Wheeler through to his rib section trying to loosen him from his harness. He was given the Purple Heart."

The aircrew used the SCR-717 to find ships of the invasion armada and avoid over flying them, in case they might be mistaken for Germans. When the other engine quit, they picked out a destroyer to ditch near.

"We prepared to ditch as we had been instructed – ass end to the front of the plane, legs around the man in front. Mae Wests were all inflated. The pilot fired a red flare for lighting. The channel was running high that but the pilot did one helluva job. He brought her in on top of one of the waves, dragged the tail, and flopped her in. We sat there as per orders. Rothwell was trying to get the dinghies inflated. The water came up around our knees and the co-pilot stuck his head back in from the blister on top of the plane and yelled, 'Get the troops out, this baby is going down!'

"Needless to say, we cleared faster than we hooked up. We got the guys who couldn't swim into the dinghies. Pustola, from Brooklyn, had his pockets full of all the pistols we had been passing up the line to throw overboard to lessen the load. Seems like he always wanted some pistols. We swam for about thirty minutes and somebody yelled, 'Ship ahoy!'

Pfc. John D. Kleinfelder in Normandy. *Courtesy of Michel De Trez*

I couldn't see any ship but it was a British destroyer or submarine patrol boat (HMS *Tarter*). We could hear the Limey's hollering, 'Shoot the bastards, they're Krauts!'

"We kept shouting, 'American paratroopers! American paratroopers!'

"I have a great warm feeling in my heart for the English. They fished us out of the Briny depths; gave us grog (we were all frozen), and extended such hospitality as was available on D-Day at very early morning (0100 a.m.)."

With the lead plane down in the Channel, the task of lighting Drop Zone 'C' fell to Lt. Roy G. Kessler's group and also the 3rd Battalion stick representing the 501st Regiment under the command of Lt. Charles M. Faith. Units scheduled to land in this area were the 506th Parachute Regiment minus its 3rd Battalion, which had a key assignment further south, and 3rd Battalion of the 501st Parachute Regiment and the Division's Headquarters personnel. Overlapping the DZ 'C' was the glider landing area known as LZ 'E', on which the two glider lifts were scheduled to drop.

Adversity continued to plague these pathfinders. The plane carrying Lt. Faith's group strayed in the approach across the Contentin Peninsula and dropped the men approximately three miles southwest of the intended landing area. Lt. Kessler's crew had, in addition to the Eureka set and several lights, an initially new radar gadget known as the 'BUPS' beacon. This had been especially prepared for the pathfinders by the British Branch Radiation Laboratories, and was used as the center point navigational aid for the entire division. All lost planes were to guide on this device and drop their loads of troopers on DZ 'C'. However, the delicate antenna was broken on landing, and the set was not functional.

Kessler's stick landed in the middle of the intended DZ and was able to set up a radar set and part of the light aids at that point, which was only one-quarter mile from the intended point for signaling. It was fortunate that two Eureka sets were part of the equipment on each drop zone because one of the men assigned to Kessler wasn't able to get his equipment in operation. PFC Terence "Salty" Harris jumped with one of the ultra-high frequency homing devices; however, he did not get it off his harness to set it in operation. German soldiers spotted him and kept him on the run.

Two sticks of the pathfinders dropped on DZ 'C' at approximately the same time. Their assignment was to prepare the landing site for the two glider lifts scheduled for 0400 A.M. and 2100 P.M.

One of the groups led by Lt. Don S. Driver of the 502nd Parachute Infantry Regiment had difficulty in orienting its position. One of the officers moved toward a farmhouse to find the correct location of his men. Nearby, a dog barked furiously. To prevent enemy troops in the area from determining his location, the officer grabbed the animal and cut his throat with a sharp knife. According to Lillyman, "This stick proceeded to the field selected for the landing zone, and with their Holophane lights, laid out the runway for the gliders. The first glider that landed was piloted by Colonel Mike Murphy and carried Brigadier General Don F. Pratt, the assistant commander of the 101st Airborne Division. The glider landed shortly before 0400 A.M. Unfortunately, one of the early gliders landed directly on top of the lights, destroying each of the carefully laid out indicators. The remaining gliders had to land in the moonlight without field markings."

Two members of Lt. Driver's stick of pathfinders related their experiences.

"The pilot must have slowed down to minimum flying speed," stated T/5 Richard Lisk. "My jump was perfect, but I had so much equipment that I landed off balance, on one foot, fracturing it."

"I crawled into a ditch beside a hedgerow. The other fellows passing by later, had to leave me to proceeds to the drop zone designated for the gliders. On being left alone, I remained quiet and hidden. I held my breath as German soldiers passed by a short time later. As they passed within arm's reach, they kicked dirt in my face. When daylight came, I destroyed my radar set. Later on, a medic came and gave me a hypo of morphine in my leg and deaden the pain. With the anesthetic action of the drug, I was able to walk. I found several glider pilots, and with them acting as scouts and points, I later found my regimental headquarters which I joined."

"I had a hard landing among the cows in a pasture just north of Vierville," said Pvt. Howard "Hic" Stiles. I had no trouble getting out of my chute. The entire stick assembled quickly. T/5 Dick Lisk injured his ankle and was left in a hedgerow. We brought in the first group of gliders, near Vierville, at approximately 0400 hours. I recall seeing General Pratt's glider crash in the hedgerow."

Three planeloads of pathfinders had been scheduled to drop as part of a team commanded by Capt. Frank L. Brown of the 501st Regiment. They were to set up their aids before the drops of the main body scheduled to land on DZ 'D'. The flight encountered sporadic flak several miles from the scheduled drop area. One of the sticks managed to hit right on the button while the other two planes jumped the men short, landing them just to the northwest of St. Come du Mont.

Somehow the Germans had sensed the fields in the Drop Zone 'D' area might be used as an airborne landing area and prepared an ambush with machineguns and mortars zeroed in on it from three sides. Flares were in a ready position for release and a large farm building had been soaked with gasoline and waited only for the application of a torch. Meanwhile the well-concealed and dug-in Germans waited in the hedgerows.

The pathfinders had been warned to avoid enemy contact if at all possible and to concentrate on their job of guiding the planes. The trailblazers came floating down to find fire playing on the fields as they landed.

Using hand grenades, one group managed to creep forward and silence two machine guns without getting hurt themselves. Flares began to pop overhead lighting the entire area so no one dared move for fear of being observed.

At the sound of more planes approaching from the west, the Germans applied the torch to the building. The holocaust lighted the entire area with its dancing flames, dwarfing any beacons the men might have lighted for the approaching planes. Because they were pinned down in the corners of the hedgerows, the pathfinders did not get the lights rigged in a 'T' and had to rely on the radar set to "home-in" its serials of troop carrier planes.

Almost half of the three-stick team of pathfinders to drop in Drop Zone 'D' were killed or captured in the early fighting and yet DZ 'D' was to receive the most concentrated drop of troopers for the entire division.

Aboard one of the planes, which dropped its pathfinders short was Lt. Albert E. Watson from the 1st Battalion of the 501st. He said, "I landed somewhat north of St. Come du Mont and collected five or six men from my stick. My group set up one pathfinder radar set."

Right: Cpl. T.K. Larsen F/501st in Normandy. *Courtesy of Mark Bando*

Far right: T/5 Richard Beaver F/501st in Normandy. *Courtesy of Mark Bando*

A member of that stick, and also one of the men collected by Lt. Watson was Corporal Joe Haller.

Joe had consumed a lot of coffee at the North Witham Airfield before taking off on D-Day night. As a result, he had to urinate during the flight across. He stood in the open door of the C-47, unzipped, and let go. The wind from the propellers blew the urine back into the plane, spraying his mortified buddies. Naturally, there was a lot of cursing and protesting.

"You guys are gonna have a lot more to worry about than a little pee!," Haller told them. Like many of the others aboard, Haller was smoking a cigarette. He began to sing a song he had heard in a western movie:

I'm smokin' my last cig-a-rette,
sing that cowboy song
I ne-ver will for-get...
I'm smokin' my last cig-a-rette.

"Shut up, you bastard!" the men shouted; they didn't want to hear that.

Joe wasn't too scared, even when violent flak began to rock the plane. Over DZ 'D', the plane banked and the first three jumpers fell out the door; they didn't even have to jump. Haller was one of them. As he fell, his Tommy gun flew down in front of his chest but he caught it. Shrapnel burst open his chest reserve chute and he grasped that desperately in his arms. He soon hit the ground and could see tracer bullets passing over him as he struggled to get out of his harness.

"The Germans must have been scared too," he later said. "They weren't far away – they could have rushed me."

Haller began to walk, went through a gap in the hedgerow and crossed a dark road.

A German voice yelled, "Halte!"

Haller answered in fluent German, "There's more of them over here – be careful!"

Haller could hear a commotion as the Germans were capturing another member of his stick. He was able to escape and rejoin his regiment after signaling in concert with Russell Walker, of the 2nd Battalion stick, whom he encountered in a large ditch. This was near St. Come du Mont.

He was one of the men carrying radar sets and had this to say: "I ran to a hedgerow after getting free of my chute and set up the Eureka radar set. It sent out a signal 'D' in Morse Code (-..). This was the signal for our drop zone. Our air transport had difficulty. It dropped our men too far apart for effectiveness."

One member of Lt. Charles Faith's misdropped 3rd Battalion stick described his experience. "We were fired on by the Germans, but not in excessive force," said Pvt. Spencer E. Everly. "We caught them off guard. The jump was all right, but I was really scared. We landed approximately two and a half miles from Carentan. I headed for the hedgerows, and began looking for other members of my stick. I located Alvin Haux, Lester Hunt, Sgt. John O'Shaughnessy, and Lt. Charles Faith. Stanley Suwarsky came down in a tree. He was shot without having the opportunity to get out of his chute."

Pvt. Leonard Newcomb, pathfinder from the 501st 2nd Battalion stick was captured. He related, "We were just leaving an area of heavy flak. The Germans had set up a lot of fire several miles west of the DZ, when the sky lit up again as the green light went on for us to jump. Like the popping of corn, the shots were going through the chute. I thought the jump was low; yet, it seemed long in getting down. I landed within fifty yards of an enemy machine gun.

"I got up and ran for the hedgerow, approximately fifteen yards distant from the position of the machine gunner. I met Red Larson and two fellows from the 3rd Battalion stick. We were able to set up radar equipment, but could not assemble together due to the heavy concentration of small arms fire from a German platoon operating near us. I watched the planes of the regiment pass overhead. The jumpers landed on the opposite side of the road from our position. We were unable to get off the fields on which we dropped. Larson had me watch the machine gun crew while he attempted to find a way out of the area, and to locate Capt. Brown, our stick leader."

"The Germans finally discovered the three of us approximately ten hours later. They had enough weapons to overpower us. I had an M-1, one fellow had a .45 caliber pistol, and the third had a carbine."

"Larson, I learned after the war, was only ten feet away from us. He stayed hidden for three or four days but our three man group became POWs."

Pfc. Robert E. Sechrist of E Company 501st landed by a hedgerow just off the DZ. He was pinned down by a German machinegun position fifty yards away and never got the chance to set up his two light sets.

The area around St. Come du Mont was ringed with fortifications and therefore had a heavy concentration of enemy troops. Several of the fields bore anti-airborne obstacles. One of the troopers who jumped with the 501st Battalion pathfinder group was Pvt. John D. Mishler, from Baker Company. His assignment was to prevent Kraut interference with the pathfinders while they set up their equipment for marking the DZ: "I came down through the top of a tree. As fourteenth man in the stick, I landed near flooded ground in the vicinity of St. Come du Mont."

"With tracers streaming low over the tall grass, I cut myself loose, and headed for the hedgerows. The radar equipment was not placed in operation by our stick. Several of our men were captured, but were released by our own men, and reached the company area prior to us."

Summarizing the work of the pathfinders on this drop zone, Captain Lillyman wrote, "The team that dropped on Drop Zone 'D' just north of Carentan, landed between the German outpost line and their main line position. This team consisted of the 501st, and the 3rd Battalion of the 506th Regiment with its attached security personnel. All three, were in a 'helluva mess', but they did a wonderful job. Credit should be given to the 440th and 441st Groups of the Troop Carrier Command. Using radar only, and no lights because of the tenuous position, forty-seven aircraft delivered their personnel to the intended DZ. This totaled more than the other two drop zones combined.

The various pathfinder teams had accomplished their missions, to the best of their abilities; this, under most trying conditions. They now awaited the main body of parachutists and glider men to become once again a part of their regular units from which they had been "on leave", to serve as vanguard of the invasion.

Above and next page: These rare pictures of 101st Airborne Pathfinders were taken from an amateur film taken with Capt. Frank Lillyman's 16mm camera, which he carried all through the war. When these pictures were filmed Lillyman was making his claim to be the first paratrooper to set foot on French soil during the invasion. *Courtesy of Michel De Trez*

PLANE #1, 502nd Parachute Infantry Regiment, 101st Airborne Division

Drop Zone 'A'

Capt. Frank I. Lillyman	HQ*	Team leader for stick #1 and 101st Div. (not pictured)

(Back row left to right)

1 Lt. Samuel McCarter	HQ*	
1 Lt. Robert S. Dickson	S-2	
Pvt. John S. McFarlen	HQ*	
Pvt. August M. Mangoni	B*	
Pvt. Bluford R. Williams	*	
Pvt. John S. Zamanakis	HQ*	Eureka operator
T/5 Owen R. Council	HQ*	
Pvt. John H. Funk	KIA	Normandy Security
S/Sgt. Thomas G. Walton	*	
Pfc. Delbert A. Jones	B*	Light team

(Front row left to right)

Pvt. Paul O. Davis	Security	
Pvt. Francis A. Rocca	C*	manifested for plane #2
Pvt. Raymond Smith	Medic	
Pfc. Frederick A. Wilhelm	*	Light team
Pvt. John G. Ott	S-2	
Pvt. Jarris C. Clark	S-2	
2 Lt. Reed Pelfrey	HQ	

(Not in picture)

Pvt. James J. Bement	Security	

PLANE #2, 502nd Parachute Infantry Regiment, 101st Airborne Division

Drop Zone 'A'

Pvt. Louis F. Banft		
T/5 Glenn B. Braddock	*	
Pvt. George C. Dagres	C	
Pvt. Wilfred Deslauriers	2*	
Pvt. Gilbert T. Driscoll	2*	
Pvt. James E. Elliott	*	
Pfc. Cifford F. Gorton	C	
Pfc. William F. Haas	Medic	
Pfc. John D. Kleinfelder	C	KIA Holland
2 Lt. Napoleon T. Lavelle	HQ	KIA
Pfc. William B. Mench	D*	
Pvt. Bernard L. Ormsbee	C	
Cpt. Henry G. Plitt	S-3	
Pvt. Francis A. Rocca	C*	actually flew in plane #1
Pfc. Ernest Stene	E*	
Pfc. Roy B. Williams	*	
Pvt. Philip Sangenario	F	
Pfc. Vincent Wallace	C	

PLANE #3, 377th Parachute Artillery Battalion, 101st Airborne Division

Drop Zone 'C'

Pvt. William H, Barton	D*	Light team
T/4 James O Detrick	A*	
Pvt. Edward D. Dulmin	A*	
Pvt. Francis G. Gunning	C*	
Pfc. Francis B. Haage	D*	
Cpl. Graham C. Ludwig	*	
T/4 John M. Murphy	HQ*	
Pfc. John B. Sample	B*	
Cpl. Michael P. Sapara	A*	
2 Lt. Robert G. Smith	HQ*	Team Leader
Cpl. Calvin C. Jackson	C/326th*	

PLANE #4, 506th Parachute Infantry Regiment, 101st Airborne Division

Drop Zone 'C'

Pfc. Robert R. Blankenship	KIA	
Pfc. Carl L. Fenstermaker	E*	
Pfc. Frederick Linacre	D	
Pvt. Charles R. Malley	F*	Acting 1st Sgt.
Cpl. Jack E. Matts	D	KIA
Pfc. Henry M. Meehan	D	
2 Lt. Rolf Michaelis	2	
Pvt. Charles H. Partlow	D*	
Pfc. Stephen Pustola	F*	
1 Lt. Gordon O. Rothwell	D*	Team Leader
Pfc. John Sherbon	D	KIA
Pfc. Lachman M. Tillman	*	
Pvt. Jerome E, Werbela	D	
Pvt. James Wheeler	2*	
Pfc. John M. White	D*	
Pfc. John W. Wright	D	
Cpl. Richard M. Wright	E*	

Lt. Rothwell's plane crashed into the English Channel and all aboard were picked up by British ships and returned to England safely.

PLANE #5, 506th Parachute Infantry Regiment, 101st Airborne Division

Drop Zone 'C'

Pfc. Walter G. Amerman		
Pvt. George H. Blain	1*	
Pvt. Leo C. Bert	C*	
Pfc. Donald W. Carter	B	KIA
Pvt. Harold V. Combs	B	
Pfc. Eugene D. Doerr	C*	
Pfc. Harold G. Duty	A*	
Pfc. Terence C. Harris	1*	KIA 11 June 1944 Carentan
1 Lt. Roy H. Kessler	A*	KIA
Pfc. Cleo W. Mers	C*	
Pvt. John Messman	A	
Pvt. Robert L. Pollard	B	
Pvt. Manderson V. Pullin	B	
Cpl. LeRoy Shalenberg	B*	
Sgt. Walter M. Skeen	B	
Pvt. George H. Slater	B	
Pvt. Fred J. Taylor	*	
Pfc. John T. Wilson	B	

Pvt. Leo C. Bert was assigned to Gen. Maxwell Taylor's bodyguard.

PLANE #6, 501st Parachute Infantry Regiment, 101st Airborne Division

Drop Zone 'C'

T/5 Henry J. Billings	HQ*	
Pfc. Lawrence R. Burgoon	I	
Pvt. William J. Dooley	I	

Plane #1 502nd Parachute Infantry Regiment, 101st Airborne Division on June 5, 1944. *Courtesy of George Koskimaki*

Plane #4, 506th Parachute Infantry Regiment, 101st Airborne Division on June 5, 1944. *Courtesy of George Koskimaki*

Plane #5, 506th Parachute Infantry Regiment, 101st Airborne Division on June 5, 1944. *Courtesy of George Koskimaki*

Plane #6, 501st Parachute Infantry Regiment, 101st Airborne Division on June 5, 1944. *Courtesy of George Koskimaki*

1 Lt. John W. Ell	H*	KIA Team Leader
Pvt. Spencer E. Everly	I*	
2 Lt. Charles M. Faith	HQ*	
S/Sgt. Chester R. Garreston		KIA
Pvt. Edmund L. Gregoire	I	
Pvt. Alvin Haux	HQ*	
Pvt. Lester Hunt	HQ*	
Pfc. Kendall C. Lewis	I	
Pvt. Michael Rofer	I*	KIA
Pvt. Ernest A. Robinson	3*	
Pvt. George L. Sarlas	3*	KIA
Pvt. Stanley S. Suwarsky	3*	KIA 6 June 1944 upon landing
Pvt. Bert V. Tadsen	I	
Pvt. Henry C. Taylor	I	

PLANE #7, 501st Parachute Infantry Regiment, 101st Airborne Division

Drop Zone 'D'

Sgt. Joe Bass	F*	KIA Sept. 1950 Korea
T/5 Richard H. Beaver	2*	
Pvt. John J. Bouska	E	
Cpt. Frank L. Brown	HQ*	
Pfc. Robert A. Howarth	D*	
2 Lt James V. Haslam	HQ	
1 Lt Joe G, McGregor	E	KIA Recogne, Belgium
Cpl. Thorwald Larsen	F*	
Cpl. Hilary J. McKenna	E	Security
Pvt. Robert J. Mileski	E	
Pvt. Leonard J. Newcomb	F*	POW
Pvt. Walter V. Olender	E	KIA
Pvt. Ralph A. Newton	F*	KIA
Pfc. Maneul Peralis	E	
Pvt. Theordore T. Pierz	E	
Pvt. Eugene L. Schuler	E	
Pfc. Robert E. Sechrist	E*	
Pfc. Harold E. Sellers	F*	KIA 6 June 1944 Normandy
Cpl. Russell G. Waller	E*	KIA Holland

PLANE #8, 501st Parachute Infantry Regiment, 101st Airborne Division

Drop Zone 'D'

Pfc. George E. Adomitis	B	KIA
Cpl. Delbert S. Brazzle	A*	KIA Holland
Pfc. Charles E. Coleman	B	
2 Lt. John H. Crow	B	Team Leader
Pvt. Alvin Daley	B	KIA
T/5 John E. Eagen	B	
Pfc. Paul H. Fletcher	B	
Pvt. Lubomir Dejanovich	*	POW
Pvt. David M. Hadley	1st Bn*	
T/5 Joe Haller	1st Bn*	Eureka operator
Pvt. Clarence J. Jack	A*	
Sgt. Warren K. McGinley	B*	
Pvt. John D. Mishler	B	Security
Pvt. John C. Ryan	B	
Sgt. John O'Shaughnessy	B*	
Pfc. Stephen Via, Jr.	B	KIA
Pvt. Thomas M. Walker	B*	
2 Lt. Albert E. Watson	A*	

PLANE #9, 506th Parachute Infantry Regiment, 101st Airborne Division

Drop Zone 'D'

Cpl. James A. Benson	3*	
Pfc. Jack L. Brown	I	
Sgt. Thayer Carlton	3*	KIA
W/O Ernest L. Dilburn	3*	
Pfc. John D. Edwards	I	
Pfc. Wilbur D. Croteau	G*	KIA
Pfc. George D. Kenfield	I*	KIA
Pfc. Edmund Lojko	HQ*	
Sgt. Sidney L. McCullum	I	
Pvt. George McMillan	I	
Pfc. John J. Monk	*	KIA
Pvt. David D. Morgan	I	
Pvt. Dell T. Ripple	3*	
Pvt. Raymond J. Schaneer	*	KIA
T/4 Louis B. Tuttle	*	MIA
2 Lt. John T. Windish	I	Team Leader
T/5 Erwin F. Zanradnik	I	

PLANE #10, 2nd BN, 505th Parachute Infantry Regiment, 82nd Airborne Division

Drop Zone 'O'

Robert Anderson		
Jim Phillips		
1 Lt. James J. Smith	505th	Team leader
Pvt. George Clark	*	
Pvt. Mickey Wargo	B	
Cpt. William S. Kirkpatrick	pilot	
Tony DeMayo	E	

(Others unknown)

PLANE #11, 3rd BN, 505th Parachute Infantry Regiment, 82nd Airborne Division

Drop Zone 'O'

T/4 Howard W. Hicks	G	
S/Sgt. Charles T. Hall	HQ	
Gail Potter	S-2	
James J. Wright		
Cpl. Bernard Hegedus	G*	Assistant Radar operator
Blasik		
Therman		
Cpl. Daniel B. Mason	H*	
Gameky		
Sgt. Fedora	I*	Assistant Radar operator
Egolf		
Ed C. Jones		
Lt. Crown		
Lt. Robert B. Bales		Team Leader

(Others unknown)

PLANE #12, 1st BN, 505th Parachute Infantry Regiment, 82nd Airborne Division

Drop Zone 'O'

Left to Right:

Sgt. Hannick	C
Ragle	C

Plane #10, 2nd Bn, 505th Parachute Infantry Regiment, 82nd Airborne Division on June 5, 1944. *Courtesy of Greg Russell*

Plane #11, 3rd Bn, 505th Parachute Infantry Regiment, 82nd Airborne Division on June 5, 1944. *Courtesy of Greg Russell*

Plane #12, 1st Bn, 505th Parachute Infantry Regiment, 82nd Airborne Division on June 5, 1944. *Courtesy of Greg Russell*

Plane #13, 3rd Bn, 507th Parachute Infantry Regiment, 82nd Airborne Division on June 5, 1944. *Courtesy of Greg Russell*

Les Allen	A	
Sgt. Elmo Jones	B	
Phil Verduce	A	
Jim Currenam	B	KIA
Meyers	C	
Pvt. Leonard Devonchuk	B	
Purcell	A	
Julius Wyngart	B	
Leslie A Finez	A	KIA
Jasper Bowman	C	
Pvt. Randy Stout	B	
Pvt. Robert M. Murphy	A*	Eureka operator
Pvt. Chuck Copping	E*	Light team
Young	A	
In door:		
Charles Burgduff		KIA
1 Lt. Michael C. Chester	A*	
Front row – Air Corps crew		
Cpt. Scott	pilot	

PLANE #13, 3rd BN, 507th Parachute Infantry Regiment, 82nd Airborne Division

Drop Zone 'T'

Standing:		
Cpl. Roy E. Neideffer		
1 Lt. Claude V. Crooks, Jr.		Assistant Team Leader
Pfc. Thomas L. Rogers	C/504th	KIA 15 June 1944
T/5 Loyd F. Durfee	H	
Pvt. Melvin E. Marshall		
Pfc. Richard C. Clark	I	
Pfc. John D. Dickinson	HQ/1/504th	POW
Pvt. Thomas J. McCarthy	A/504th	
Cpl. Alexander F. Turlo	G	
Sgt. William E. Consolvo		Eureka Operator
Pvt. Milton F. Nielson	HQ	
Kneeling:		
1 Lt. James H. Goethe	A/504th	
T/4 Paul B. Thore		Eureka Operator
Pvt. James S. Carper		
Pvt. John G. Saris		
Pvt. James K. McCormick		KIA
Pfc. Robert E. Kelley	H	
Pfc. Edward G. Miller		
Seated:		
1 Lt. John T. Joseph		Team Leader
Unknown	Air Crew	
Cpt. Minor	Pilot	
Unknown	Air Crew	
Unknown	Air Crew	
Unknown	Air Crew	
Pfc. William L. Gray	B/504th	KIA 6 June 1944 Normandy (Not in picture)

PLANE #14, 2nd BN, 507th Parachute Infantry Regiment, 82nd Airborne Division

Drop Zone 'T'

Pvt. Curry M Adderton	HQ/2/504th	
Pfc. Walter E. Chaney	F/504th	
Pvt. Edward W. Endsley	B/504th	
Pvt. Bernard G. Shipton	HQ/504th	
Pvt. Michael Evanick	F/504th	POW
1 Lt. Charles Ames		
1 Lt. Ralph McGill		
Sgt. Rolland J. Duff		Eureka Operator
Turner	F	
James R. Conroy	H	
Cpt. E.G. McElry	9th Troop Carrier Intelligence Observer	
Lt. Carl Jones	Navigator/Radar operator (door wearing helmet)	

(Others unknown)

PLANE #15, 1st BN, 507th Parachute Infantry Regiment, 82nd Airborne Division

Drop Zone 'T'

Front Row Left to Right:		
T/4 William O. Armstrong		
Thomas E. Munden		
T/5 Vincent Brophy		
John Despot		Medic
Pfc. Zigmund Hojnowski		
Chalmer D. Hanson	B	
Paul E. Pachowka		
Fred L Burns	C	
John C. Mortzfeldt	A/504th	
1 Lt. Charles R. O'Brien, Jr		Team Leader
Back Row Left to Right:		
William R. Wolf	HQ/1	
T/5 Robert C. Mitchell	HQ/1	
Unknown		
Pvt. John D. Dickson	HQ/1	
Jones H. Warren		
Pfc. Unknown		
Robert E. Olen		
Sgt. J. Morris Thompson	A	
John R. Bergendahl		
1 Lt. Quinton P. Sunday		Team Leader Not pictured

PLANE #16, 1st BN, 508th Parachute Infantry Regiment, 82nd Airborne Division

Drop Zone 'N'

Reclining:		
Unknown		
Seated:		
Pfc. Nicholas Trevino		Light team
Unknown	504th	
Unknown		
Pfc. Cipriano Gamez	C	Light team
Unknown		
Pfc. Paul Demciak		Medic
Pfc. Donald E. Krause	B	Assistant Eureka Operator
Kneeling:		
Pfc. Wilburn L. Stutler	C	NCO for Light team
Pfc. J.T. Barkley		Light team
Unknown		
Pvt. James H. Weinerth	B	Eureka Operator
Unknown		
Pvt. A.B. Cannon	A	Security

Plane #14, 2nd Bn, 507th Parachute Infantry Regiment, 82nd Airborne Division on June 5, 1944. *Courtesy of Greg Russell*

Plane #15, 1st Bn, 507th Parachute Infantry Regiment, 82nd Airborne Division on June 5, 1944. *Courtesy of Greg Russell*

Plane #16, 1st Bn, 508th Parachute Infantry Regiment, 82nd Airborne Division on June 5, 1944. *Courtesy of Greg Russell*

Plane #17, 2nd Bn, 508th Parachute Infantry Regiment, 82nd Airborne Division on June 5, 1944. *Courtesy of Greg Russell*

Standing:

Gilliam		Radio-air crew
G. Wilger		Co-pilot
Unknown	504th	
Cpl. Roy L. Smith		NCO for Security team
N. Herro		Navigator
Unknown		Air crew
Cpt. Miles		Pilot
2 Lt. R.J. Weaver	HQ/1	Team Leader

In Door:

Unknown	Air crew

Unknowns:

Capt. Neal L. McRoberts	505th Plane #16	
Cpl. Elijah D. Moore		NCO for Eureka team
Pvt. Theodore F. Bossert		Eureka Operator
Pvt. Willie E. Smith	A	Light team
Pfc. Augusta Labata	KIA	Light team
Pfc. Joseph L. Deardorff		Security
Pfc. John Sevitz	HQ/1	Security
Pfc. Raymond C. Kurtz	KIA	Security
2 Lt. Elmer Stoll	KIA	Assitant Team Leader
Pvt. Willard H. Davis		Assitant Eureka Operator
Pfc. Amos R. Cundiff	A/504th	
Pfc. William J. Hannigan	H/504th	

PLANE #17, 2nd BN, 508th Parachute Infantry Regiment, 82nd Airborne Regiment

Drop Zone 'N'

Seated:

2 Lt. R. Perez		Air Crew
2 Lt. L. Vohs		Air Crew
2 Lt. Elbert F. Hamilton	KIA	Assistant Team Leader
1 Lt. C. Gaudio		Pilot
2 Lt. Lloyd L. Polette, Jr.	KIA	Team Leader
Unknown		Air Crew
Ssgt. Unknown		Air Crew

Kneeling:

Sgt. Charles P. Katsanis	D/504th	
Pvt. Harold Jessup		
Pfc. Robert L. Seale		
Cpl. Earnest L. King		KIA
Pvt. Fred J. Infanger	E	
Pfc. Murray E. Daly	D	KIA
Pvt. John P. Perdue	D	KIA Holland
Pfc. Carl W. Jones		KIA

Standing:

Pvt. Stanton H. Messenbrink	E
Pvt. Robert L. Andreas	E
Pvt. John G. Gerard	
Pfc. Beverly J. Moss	
Pvt. Norman C. Willis	E
Pfc. Nick Forkupa	I/504th
Unknown	504th

In Door:

2 Lt. Thomas A. Murphy	HQ/3/504th	POW

Unknowns:

T/5 David Giblin		
Pfc. Sidney G. Taylor		
Pvt. Clarence N. Billings		KIA
Pvt. Arthur M. Lawrence		
Pvt. Edward G. Ozbolt		KIA
Pvt. Lemual B. Parrish		
Pvt. Eddie H. Livingston	I/504th	POW
Pvt. John P. Tornosky	I/504th	

PLANE #18, 3rd BN, 508th Parachute Infantry Regiment, 82nd Airborne Division

Drop Zone 'N'

Seated:

Unknown		Air Crew
Unknown		
Unknown		
Unknown		
Unknown		
Kneeling:		
Unknown		
Unknown		
Unknown		
Unknown		
Pfc. Arnold H. Martin	KIA	Security team
Pfc. Fayette O. Richardson	H	Eureka operator
Unknown		
Pvt. Ralph W. Nicholson	KIA	Extra
Unknown	504th	

Standing:

2 Lt. Edward J. Czenpinski	KIA	Assistant Team Leader
Pfc. Warren C. Jeffers	I	Light team
T/5 Francis M. Lamoureaux	G	Eureka operator
Pfc. Charles H. Rogers	KIA	Extra
Unknown		
Pvt. Eric Stott	HQ/3	Assistant Eureka operator
Cpl. Charles F. Calvert		NCO for light team
Unknown		
Sgt. Robert V. Barbiaux	G	Team Sergeant
2 Lt. Gene H. Williams	KIA	Team Leader

Unknowns:

Pvt. Danzil C. Rollins		Assistant Eureka operator
Pfc. Walter W. Harrelson	KIA	Light team
Pvt. Joseph F. Brumbaugh		Light team
Pvt. John P. Delury		Light team
Pvt. John F. Kimmel		Light team
Pvt. Roscoe H. Walker		NCO for security
Pfc. Joseph W. Arsenault		Security
Pfc. John E. Sternesky	I	Security
Pvt. James H. Daugherty		Security
Pvt. Thomas W. Lindsey		
Pvt. William F. Lee		
Pvt. Hal A. Murdock	504th	POW
Pvt. John H. Baldassar	H/504th	KIA 27 Sept. 1944 Holland
Pvt. Cicero J. Parchman	G/504th	POW
Pvt. Henry S. Pawlings	G/504th	KIA 6 June 1944 Normandy
Pvt. John R. Rigapoulos	H/504th	KIA 20 Sept. 1944 Holland

Plane #18, 3rd Bn, 508th Parachute Infantry Regiment, 82nd Airborne Division on June 5, 1944. *Courtesy of Greg Russell*

Plane #19, 502nd Parachute Infantry Regiment, 101st Airborne Division on June 5, 1944. *Courtesy of George Koskimaki*

Plane #20, 377th Para. Arty. Bn./326th Abn. Engr. Bn., 101st Airborne Division. *Courtesy of George Koskimaki*

PLANE #19, 502nd Parachute Infantry Regiment, 101st Airborne Division

Drop Zone 'C'

Pvt. Henry J. Bohlcke	*	
Pfc. William G. Casey	G*	
Pvt. Dominick Cherico	E	KIA
1 Lt. Don S. Driver	*	Team Leader
Pfc. Troy S. Estes	E	
Pvt. Lawrence F. Hall	E	
Pvt. Harold D. Locke	E	
T/5 Richard R. Lisk	*	Eureka operator
T/5 Clifford J. MacDowell	*	
Pvt. William G. Netterwold	*	
Pvt. David C. Parks	*	
Pvt. James H. Perkins	*	
Pfc. Cleo G. Reed	E	
Pfc. Howard Stiles	H*	
T/5 Hugh W. Selby	*	
2 Lt. James W. Tolar	E	

PLANE #20, 377th Para. Arty. Bn./326th Abn. Engr. Bn., 101st Airborne Division

Drop Zone 'C'

Standing Left to Right:

Pfc. John J, Hosta	D*	
Pvt. Saul B. Sancedo	B*	
Pfc. Louis DiGaetano	C*	KIA Bastogne
Pvt. Arthur L. Brooks	D*	
Pvt. Albert A. Koupa	C*	
T/5 Donald N. Green	A*	
Pvt. Norman D. Gannon	Medic	
T/5 Jerrold J. Quinn	B	
Cpl. Vincent L. Cart	HQ*	
1 Lt. Lawrence G. Hensley	HQ*	KIA Team Leader

Kneeling Air Crew:

1 Lt. Paul Egan	Pilot
1 Lt. Richard Young	Co-Pilot
1 Lt. Fern Murphy	Navigator
S/Sgt. Jack Buchanan	Crew Chief

Notes: Three other members of the 504th jumped with the pathfinders of the 508th but it is unknown which plane the flew in:

Pvt. Joseph W. Manfredi	E/504th	KIA 14 June 1944 Normandy
Pvt. Joseph A. Byrne	H/504th	KIA 17 June 1944 Normandy
Pvt. Bryon L. Peterson	504th	KIA Normandy

101st Airborne Provisional Pathfinder Group in England, summer of 1944. *Courtesy of George Blain via Mark Bando*

SOUTHERN FRANCE - August 15, 1944

In preparation for the upcoming invasion of Southern France teams of one officer and nine enlisted men from each of the 509th and 551st Parachute Infantry and the 550th Glider Infantry Battalions were sent to Marcigliana, south of Rome, for pathfinder training. They were trained by pathfinder Air Corps crews and veteran pathfinders who participated in the Normandy invasion a few months before. Their month long training was supervised by a lieutenant from the 505th Parachute Infantry Regiment, 82nd Airborne who had jumped into Normandy with the pathfinders.

Pvt. Henry Filipczak of Co. G, 517th Parachute Infantry remembers being assigned to the pathfinders: "One afternoon early in August, Capt. Hooper (Company Commander) called me into his tent and asked if I would accept an assignment. He briefly stated what the assignment was, not to be vague, but he himself wasn't fully knowledgeable. I assume that all thirty troopers and three lieutenants were asked in the same manner. I agreed, and went back to tell my close buddies I'd be leaving shortly. Within a couple of hours we were all on trucks, finally arriving at a military airport. We all assembled, briefly got acquainted, and each group and officer went to a different location on the remote part of the airfield. The airfield was primarily for transport aircraft, but did have some fighter planes also. Our uniforms were plain khaki for training, which lasted about ten days, as follows. Early morning rise, exercises, some limited running, then to our training. We broke up into two five man groups, each doing the same repetitious training, mainly as a back up for each group should we become separated after our jump. Each group was assigned ten or twelve panels (about two feet x twelve to fourteen feet) to lay out in a prescribed arrangement. These were for visual guidance for the main body of aircraft. We did this twenty to forty times a day for about three days. Display and timing were our main objective. Each trooper had a pattern to cover and we rotated these assignments until we got it down pat. On the fourth day each group was given a radio, antenna and battery pack to get familiar with the radio was only a transmitter (not receiver) for aircraft guidance to the DZ. We did radio set-up fifteen to twenty times a day, again each trooper was totally familiar with the complete procedure, we then started back with the panels and radio set-up until our lieutenant was satisfied with the complete procedure and timing."

"About the eighth day we united with the 1st and 2nd Battalion troopers and were taken to another part of the airfield to meet our British counterparts. We had a great time, played some volleyball and they absolutely trounced each of our teams. We were later driven back and separated once again into our initial groups. The next day we jumped from the back of slow moving trucks to simulate a jump separation and then proceed to set-up our panels and radio, we did this several times. The following morning, August 14th, we did some limited training, ran a little that afternoon, had dinner and just set around. About eight o'clock a truck pulled up, unloaded a fifty-five gallon drum with cans of ice cold beer. Our lieutenant called us together and told us that our invasion take-off time was 2 a.m. (August 15th). Have a good time, don't get drunk, write your letters, and be ready by 1 a.m. Needless to say we had a glorious time and each trooper took a couple of beers to jam into his backpack. At 1 a.m. we loaded onto a truck with all our equipment (panels, radio, battery), rifle, only essentials, left behind the rest."

A week before the Southern France invasion a team of engineers specially trained in camouflage came through the paratroops areas. One platoon went through at a time to get their jump uniforms and equipment painted. A box was put over a mans head and the team spray painted his jump suit in colors of green and black. Equipment and weapons were laid out to the side and two guys with spray guns painted them. It was quick, but the effect was very good. When the paint dried small U.S. flags were sewn onto the upper left sleeves of the jump jacket. During the jump the flag was covered by means of an issue sock having the foot cut off worn as an armband. At daybreak the sock was to be removed.

The airborne invasion of Southern France began about 0100 on the morning of August 15, when nine C-47 aircraft carrying 121 pathfinders took off from Marcigliana Airfield directly north of Rome in three serials of three planes each. Three teams were to drop on each of the three DZs around Me Luy. Favored by good weather, they reached France exactly on schedule and approximately on course, some two and a half hours later. However, over the coast of the Riviera, the planes encountered heavy fog, which covered the entire area. Visibility was less than a half-mile, and there was no moon.

The lead serial carrying the teams of the 509th and 551st Parachute Infantry and 550th Glider Infantry Battalions lost their way and circled back to sea to make a second run. After circling for about half an hour one aircraft carrying the 509th team dropped its pathfinder and returned home. They landed over a wide area from Frejus to Grasse. The other two aircraft became separated after that, one dropped its troops about 0400 hours. The last team jumped at 0415 hours on the sixth run on the target. Lost in the woods and far from the objective, none of the three teams were able to reach the Le Muy area in time to act as pathfinders.

The second serial was to drop its pathfinders from the 517th Parachute Regimental Combat Team at 0328 hours on DZ 'A'. They landed in the woods three and a half miles east of the drop zone and just east of Le Muy itself. A two-minute jump delay would have put them right on target. To make matters worse they were attacked upon landing and spent awhile fighting the assault. They arrived at the drop zone at approximately 1630 hours where they set up a Eureka beacon, a Bups beacon, and a 'T' panel which was of assistance to the afternoon mission for the area.

The third serial consisted of pathfinders of the British 1st Independent Parachute Platoon landing to mark the DZs for the British 2nd Parachute Brigade.

At the airfield at Marcigliana 1st Lt. Dan A. DeLeo, the leader of the 509th team, glanced at his luminous watch it was 1255 a.m., nearly time to board his C-47. DeLeo's blackened-faced team would have less than sixty minutes to reconnoiter the ground and plant portable beacon signals on the drop zone to guide in the original flight of 396 troop transport planes.

DeLeo, in nearly two years of combat duty, had led a twenty-nine man raiding party ninety miles behind German lines in Tunisia on Christmas Eve in 1942. They had the mission of blowing up a key bridge at a hamlet named El Djem. This railroad bridge was used to help supply the German *Afrikakorps*. It was said to be a suicide mission of, which they were told to get back the best way they could.

In September 1943, he and the rest of the 509th jumped some twenty-five to thirty miles behind German lines at Salerno, Italy, to relieve pressure on the U.S. 5th Army, which was on the verge of being thrown back into the sea.

While speaking with the lieutenant colonel who would be flying him to southern France, DeLeo mentioned that his pilots had misdropped him on earlier missions. The pilot dismissed DeLeo's fear by confidently telling him that he was "absolutely positive" that he would drop the pathfinders "right on the money" in France. "And if I miss your DZ," said the pilot, "I'll send you a case of the best scotch money can buy!"

His pathfinders were loaded down with seventy pounds or more of combat gear, DeLeo and his men waddled up a short ladder and through the open doorway of the C-47. Wedging himself into a bucket seat, he was careful not to glance toward one end of the cabin. He wanted to avoid 'seeing' two AWOL men who were stowing away on the aircraft in order to make the jump into Southern France. Neither was authorized to go along.

Sgt. Hugh Roberts of the 551st team remembers, "We had been training for two months for the pathfinder mission. On 14 August we reported for the final briefing at 2000 and got the final weather report and had a talk by the officer who was taking us in, concerning how careful we had to be. Everyone was feeling good and we were all ready for the jump. I started to get that feeling, as always before a jump."

"We reported to the plane at 2100 and they gave us cocoa, as it was getting cool. I was thinking of all the people I ever knew and was wondering what they were doing. We loaded onto the plane at 2345, take off was 2400. Everyone was getting that far-off look in their eyes. I gat sick and heaved in the plane just before we hit South France. Stood up and got ready as we came over the coast. We went in over the DZ but didn't go. Again we went over the DZ and didn't go. Everyone got mad as hell – we had been standing up for a long time. Back out to sea – that makes three times."

"Then all hell broke loose. It looked like small arms fire but some of the boys said there was flak. By this time I would have taken anywhere else in the world but here. The plane was sure having trouble. The red light went off and we thought we had been hit. The plane picked up speed to about 140 and all of a sudden both lights came on together. What a helluva feeling came over me. I heard the Lt. shout, 'Let's go!' Being the last man, I had no one to push me. I wanted to pray but didn't know what to say. It was so dark we could just make out the door. The man in front of me was gone and then I was out."

The pathfinders of the 551st would fly in three different aircraft. In the first would be twelve enlisted men and two officers. The second aircraft carried Capt. Tims Quinn, Frank Serio and one other enlisted man. The third carried Lt. Milt Hill.

Capt. Tims Quinn recalls, "Frank Serio may have been with me on the plane. There were three of us, including an enlisted man. Before the jump, Frank and I were lying there on the ground at the airfield, looking up at the sky, and I read him a selection out of the *Book of 101 Best Poems* called 'I Have a Rendezvous With Death.' He didn't think to much of that. He said, 'Let's be serious for a while. If anything happens to me, I want you to contact my wife.'"

As Lt. DeLeo's aircraft neared the French coast just before 0300, he stood in the doorway, gazing toward the murky terrain outline of the Riviera. He felt a surge of alarm: the entire region was shrouded in a thick blanket of fog. Landmarks he had studied on sand table mock-ups for countless hours could not be detected.

A few minutes later German anti-aircraft fire opened up on the aircraft sending shrapnel ripping through the fuselage. The crew chief yelled to DeLeo, "The pilot can't make out a thing on the ground! He's going to circle out to sea and take another crack at it."

Pvt. John Devanie was a pathfinder of the 509th. He is armed with a M-1928A-1 Thompson Submachine gun with front grip. *Courtesy of Michel De Trez*

The pilot tried two more times to locate the DZ, drawing anti-aircraft each time. On the third try the crew chief yelled, "He can't find the goddamned DZ! You'll have to jump now!"

DeLeo turned to his men, who had been standing up hook up read to go for almost thirty minutes, and yelled, "Okay, let's go!" DeLeo turned and jumped out the door. Upon his parachute opening he felt a searing pain and lost consciousness. A piece of shrapnel had grazed his head, ripped off his helmet, and caused blood to stream down his face.

He woke up a while later to learn he had landed in a tree twelve feet above the ground. As he tried to free himself, one of his men, Charles McDonald walked up to him in the dark. McDonald whispered "Lafayette!" DeLeo gave the countersign response, "Democracy".

McDonald quickly cut his leader down and noticed all the blood on his face and uniform and remarked, "Damn, you're a hell of a looking mess!"

DeLeo responded, "Yeah I guess I am, I was knocked out, but I think the shrapnel only grazed my head. I'm ready to go."

Though dazed by his experience and nursing a three-inch superficial scalp wound, DeLeo was quickly able to determine that he and his men had been dropped many miles away from their DZ. Upon learning his true location, DeLeo threw his hands up in disgust and said, "The Air Corps has done it to me again – but this time it's going to cost them a case of Scotch."

Pvt. Charles Petty recalled: "Fourteen paratroops made our pathfinder team. I, Charles Petty was one of them along with Armstad, Baum, Culture, Devanie, Houghton, Justice (KIA), McGee, Sweetitz (KIA), Treskowski, McDonald, Rondeau,

Saiz, and our team leader, Lt. DeLeo. Our pathfinder equipment consisted of a Eureka radar device and a dozen signal lights mounted on tripod, which were used to form a 'T' pattern on the ground to indicated the directions of flights to pilots. McDonald was the one troop chosen to jump with the Eureka. The rest of us carried the tripod and the signal lights in addition to his own weapons and ammunition. I, like many of us decided to discard the reserve parachute. It would be an item less to jump with, it would serve no purpose anyhow, we were gonna jump at such a low altitude! Although an order was issued for all paratroops flying over the sea to wear a Mae West, I didn't wear one. I think we left them in the aircraft. I carried a .45, an M-1 rifle, two ammo bandoleers and many packs of Lucky Strikes in two bandoleers I had sewn inside my jump jacket. In addition to the troopers of the Pathfinder team, there were two stowaways on board the airplane – Sgt. Emanuel Serano and 1st Sgt. James Prettyman. Serano was the buddy of our commander, Dan DeLeo, he had participated in the parachute

Below: Sgt. Richard Robb a pathfinder of the 517th PIR He carries a Holophane light under his reserve parachute and a signal panel on his right side. *Courtesy of Michel De Trez*

Right: Pvt. Charles Petty a pathfinder of the 509th at Marcigliana airfield, a few hours before take off for Southern France. *Courtesy of Michel DeTrez*

raid against El Djem Bridge in Tunisia and had been captured, escaped, and spent fourteen months with an Italian partisan band raiding German installations. Somehow, he showed up at the airbase where we were training. Prettyman was not a qualified parachutist, he was attached to our team in an administrative capacity. The two sergeants begged the lieutenant to let them come along on the mission and they wouldn't take 'no' for an answer. Since DeLeo couldn't give them official permission, both men decided to stowaway in the airplane while DeLeo 'happened' to be looking in another direction. The airplane was in total blackout except for a soft blue light in the ceiling of the fuselage, which would give each of us a fierce appearance in our camouflage jump suits with blackened faces. Once airborne, except for the sounds of the aircraft's engines all was quiet, nobody spoke. I looked at my buddies around me and wondered how many of us would live to see the sunset? Eventually, some of the guys began to doze off and I, also began to feel sleepy. I finally fell asleep and was awakened by the Air Corps crew chief who was moving up and down the aisle. Moments later we neared the coast, the crew chief shouted, 'stand in the door'. DeLeo made a half turn and crouched in the exit door as the rest of us shuffled forward to close the gaps between jumpers. Our eyes were fixed on the red light in the exit door knowing that when it changed to green it would be the signal to bail out. As we flew over the coast the enemy's anti-aircraft guns opened up on us. I expected the red light to turn green anytime, but it remained red. Suddenly the aircraft went into a sharp turn which threw us to the side of the fuselage. It was almost impossible to stay on our feet. The crew chief hollered, 'we can't make out a thing on the ground, we are going to circle out to sea and make another crack at it!' Twice more we circled each time drawing a barrage of flak, I remember McGee yelling: 'Let's get the hell out of here' and the lieutenant shouting he couldn't see any thing out in the thick fog. On the third pass the aircraft went into a steep glide and someone shouted: 'We are going to ditch,' and I closed my eyes and prayed holding tight to the rosary my mother had given me. Finally after what seemed like an eternity, the aircraft began to level off, but the force of the gravity was so great it forced us to the ground of the airplane. I grabbed the anchor line and held for dear life as the plane returned to level flight. Finally, the red light went green and I heard DeLeo shouting; 'Okay, let's go", and go we did!'"

"After my chute opened, I came crashing down in a tree and there I hung. I was able to unhook my rifle and my pathfinder equipment and dropped them to the ground. I managed with some difficulty to reach my switchblade knife and cut loose the parachute harness. I then climbed down and found out I was in a wooded area full of tall pine trees certain this was not the DZ. I called out in a low voice the password 'Lafayette' but got no answer. I was alone behind enemy lines! As dawn approached, the fog began to lift. I climbed the tree to retrieve my parachute. I wrapped it around my Pathfinder equipment and hid everything in some thick underbrush nearby. As I made my way down the side of the hill I could hear heavy artillery far off in the distance, I knew then that the invasion along the coast had begun and I immediately removed the sock covering the American flag I had sewn to my sleeve of my jacket. By mid-morning we were six and during the afternoon we joined up with the rest of our team. We found everyone to be okay, except DeLeo who had sustained a fractured skull when he was struck by a shell fragment from the enemy's anti-aircraft fire during the jump. We found that we had been dropped some twenty-five miles from our intended DZ. The Germans had patrols looking for us, but in most cases we saw them first and avoided them when ever we could. The next day we were joined by a few members of the French underground resistance and a couple days later we arrived at the small village of Tanneron where we decided to rest for a few hours. Suddenly, one of our French guides shouted: 'Les boches sont la.' The krauts were by a half mile leading to the village. DeLeo quickly assembled the team and we set up an ambush and waited for the approaching Germans. We allowed them to come within point blank range before opening fire. In two or three minutes it was all over, and the krauts who weren't down surrendered. Serano was wounded in the leg by gunfire. The next day we left the village with our prisoners and heartbroken, one of our buddies, McDonald, had to be left behind. He had a case of fever, which turned out to be malaria, He could no longer travel with us so we left him in the hands of a friendly French family in the wooded area up the hill. DeLeo told him to hold on to his .45 and get rid of everything else. He was given civilian clothes and before we left him, each one of us went by his bedside and shook his hand promising that we would come back to get him out. Along the road while we stopped near a house to take a rest some children came out and set with me. I gave one of the little girls one of my D-ration chocolate bars, in return she gave me a small medallion which I attached to my dog tags. Suddenly high explosive shells began exploding all around the immediate area. I got the little girl down in a ditch on the side of the road with me and there we stayed until it stopped. I later found out that on the medallion was written: 'Toi et moi, un abri pour deux' which means: 'You and me, a shelter for both', I kept it to these days. The prisoners were told that there would be no turning back, no playing around, and I think we scared them. When later the GIs of an infantry division took over the prisoners, one of them gave me a little foxhole rosary thanking me for not having killing him. I kept that little thing all though the war and it remained in the pocket of my jump jacket until today. While retuning to friendly territory, Lt. DeLeo organized a rescue team composed of troopers Baum, Saiz, and Trzeskowski, three British paratroopers and a French resistance fighter by the name of Mario. They made their way through enemy lines and brought McDonald back safely. By then, our pathfinder team was disbanded and we all retuned to our assigned units. When I rejoined my company I found out I had a new company commander, I was told that Captain Miller and sixteen of my comrades had been dropped before their airplane cleared the coast. I had returned just in time for more action as the Battalion was preparing for an attack against the castle of La Napoule where the Germans were still holding on. It turned out to be one of the heaviest casualties attack the Battalion has sustained throughout the war. From my buddies of the pathfinder team, I never heard of any of them again, I later learned DeVanie was severely wounded during the attack, McGee also, and I too was wounded during the bloody battle. When I returned to the Battalion six to seven weeks later, it was stationed at a foothill in the French Alps."

Capt. Tims Quinn recalls, "We boarded the plane at about 2400. I jumped with an artillery unit that was attached to the 509th, it could have been the 488th or the 456th, and I didn't know anyone in that group. I didn't speak to them and they didn't speak to me. It was foggy and cloudy on the way in and a few tracers were coming up. The plane went over three times and each time we tried to get this bundle out the door but it was stuck in the opening. The third time, the pilot came back and said it had to go that time or he would take us back. Then he tipped the wings over hard and we heaved and out the bundle went. I was the last one out."

"I don't remember anything except a big opening shock, and I realized that they hadn't slowed the plane down. It stripped off everything I had: musette bag, submachine gun, pistol, canteen, grenades, everything. I got on the ground and all I had left was my compass and a trench knife in my boot. I stumbled around in the dark for a while, hit a big rock fence, plowed through that and it sounded like I had knocked down every rock in South France. After things quieted down I got up and tippied through the woods and first thing you know, someone was behind me saying 'psst – psst.' I realized that these were the people I had jumped with, and we kind of went along together. I got to the road about daylight, and we didn't know where we were but we could hear a lot of shooting as we headed for the sound; it had to be where some of our people had landed. On the way I saw a few Germans that had been killed and one that was badly wounded. I thought I would hate him and want to kill him but I didn't; I felt sorry for him because he was hurting. He was motioning for me to give him a cigarette and I got one out of my pocket and lit it for him."

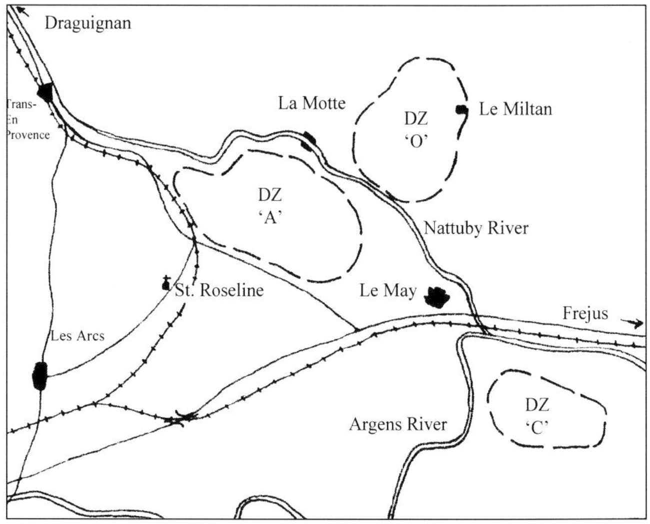

Drop zones 'A', 'C', and 'O' around the town of Le Muy in Southern France.

"Then I got hold of a gun. There was three of us who jumped in advance of the battalion so that we would be down there, reconnoiter the ground and be able to guide them into defensive positions as soon as they hit. Some of the people there on the ground near where I landed resented it because I wouldn't get into a firefight along with part of the 509th. They wanted me to go help dislodge some Germans in a little town that wasn't even in our sector but I wouldn't do it because I had the job to do for our battalion."

"Anyway, we were there to greet the battalion but there were only two of us, me and the enlisted man. The battalion came in and it was a good thing that most of the Task Force missed their planned DZs because the Germans knew we were coming and had brought in flak guns and had most of our intended DZs well covered. Evidently that was the most publicized jump ever."

Sgt. Hugh Roberts of the 551st recalls, "The opening shock was the worst I ever had. The plane never slowed down. Then everything was quiet. I could make out a few things on the ground and could see a chute in front of me. It seemed to take a lifetime to get to the ground. I think they dropped us at about 1,700 feet, instead of the planned 500. I hit on the side of a little hill. I jumped to my feet, got my gun ready and got out of my chute. The first thing I thought of as I looked around was, 'So this is France.'"

"There had been a lieutenant, myself and eleven riflemen on the plane and I was the only communications man. Some of us had submachine guns. At no time did all of us get together on the ground. That first day, we ran into the lieutenant and there were six of us altogether."

"I landed on the side of a shale hill and there were some pine trees. Just before we landed I could hear the air raid whistles up and down the valley. Then we went into cover and I lay there for a while, just taking it easy. I took an azimuth with my compass on the moon and stars and I said, 'Shit, we're way off. We are nowhere near where we are suppose to be.' I decided at that point that the radar I was carrying had to go. It had a built-in destruct cartridge and a pin you could pull. But that would have brought the Germans, so we took out the explosive charge and smashed the set with a rock. Most of the chutes were in the trees and we left them."

"Then I saw 'Duke' Spletzer and we talked, and then we met another guy but we didn't know him. He had a broken leg or ankle so we dragged him under a tree and left him. It had gone from 0300 until almost dawn. 'Duke' and I just lay there until daylight because we knew we were lost. At daybreak we could hear the Germans shouting to one another and discovered they were putting outpost around the anti-aircraft guns they had in the hills around us. They were changing guards. Our little group was going to shoot them but I said, 'Jesus Christ, don't shoot. We're in enough trouble as it is. Don't shoot nobody.' 'Duke' was a rifleman and could speak German."

They cautiously slipped away, and as they resumed their trek they ran into a lieutenant and three others who jumped from their C-47. A short distance away, an enemy machine gun suddenly opened fire on the six men. Spletzer, Roberts and another man dashed off in one direction, the other three scattered in other directions. The other three would never be seen again by Roberts and Spletzer.

Pvt. Roger P. Carqueville of the 551st team recalled, "We didn't drop until 0400 on the 15th. We were scheduled to rendezvous with a diversionary force of bombers over Corsica and then cross the beach at approximately 0400. We were supposed to stand up and hook up as we crossed the coastline, and stand there for about nine minutes, and according to our briefing we would then go over this mountain and then they would drop the aircraft sharply, get over the DZ and we would make the jump."

"But it didn't work out that way. We were loaded down with equipment. Sgt. Hugh Roberts had the radar set and the rest of us had Halaphane lights and tripods and batteries plus our rations, ammunition, and weapons. This bird colonel from the Troop Carrier Command (the bastard still owes us a case of Scotch. 'If I don't get you guys in the right place, I will buy you a case of Scotch.') So we crossed the beach, the red light went on, we stood up, hooked up, checked our equipment, and we stood there and stood there, for damned near forty-five minutes. By that time we were dragging – we could hardly stand up. We were standing there all weighted down and it got to the point where our legs were giving out and our backs were giving out, and finally, in sheer desperation I think, the green light came on. I was at the back of the stick and all I know is that I wanted to get out of that plane."

"I came crashing down through the trees on the side of a mountain. There was a sliver of a moon and you couldn't see much. I cut myself out of my harness because my chute was hung up in a tree and the balls of my feet just touched the ground. Dawn broke and it was obvious that we were nowhere near the DZ; then I heard voices but couldn't recognize them as American, French, or German. I was alone, and had pulled my chute down out of the tree and stuck it in some bushes along with the Holophane light because it was of no use to me now. Why I even had the Holophane light I don't know, since it was to be a day jump. Our mission was to set up the DZ, and the radar set on the ground was called the 'Eureka', and the one in the plane was 'Rebecca'. We all had practiced with them. I don't remember what the signal was, but we were supposed to code every so many seconds, then pause and code again. The Rebecca in the plane could pick up the signal quite a way out."

He didn't know it at the time but he had landed eighteen miles from his intended drop zone. He was looking around in the dark, looking for his teammates. Stumbling around in the dark after a while he decided to bury his Eureka beacon, which he had been carrying around. He then headed south towards the beaches along the Cote d'Azur where the sea invasion was coming. He met another paratrooper, who was unknown to him along the way.

Lt. Milt Hill the HQ Co. XO recalls his jump: "I jumped from a plane with men who were not from our outfit. The may have been from the 509th Battalion. We dropped at about 0200 and I was to go to where the 551st would be landing that afternoon and set up firing positions for our machine guns, mortars and so fourth. Then, when the battalion landed, I could direct the men to those positions. Unfortunately, when I got on the ground I found I had lost my carbine and .45 on the opening shock. I think the Army Air Corps dropped us at about 150 feet because I didn't oscillate but once before I hit. Since I had no weapon. I took out my hand grenade, pulled the pin, but held onto the handle. I figured if I got into trouble I would just drop it and run like hell."

"Then I found some of the men who had dropped with me and they gave me a .45. We started to move around in the dark and came across this little hut. We knocked on the door, then we could hear voices inside and they were speaking French so we went inside. None of us could speak French, but those people were real happy when they saw the American flags on our shoulders. I pulled out a map and showed them where we were supposed to be, then I pointed at the ground and made them understand that they were supposed to show us on the map just where we were. Well, we were about fifteen miles from our DZ and very near the coast. One of the men who lived there seemed to be with the Resistance or whatever, and he agreed to take us to the DZ, or so we thought."

"So he started leading us along and we did OK until that afternoon. We were then working our way carefully along a valley and here came the 551st flying over us. They were going in to the DZ, and here we were, nowhere near the area. So two days later we finally caught up with the battalion. To this day I can't remember who the other men were. They may have been from the 517th Regiment or the 509th Battalion. I got to Le Muy just after the 551st had taken Draguignan. Shroeder had been shot through the lung. Anyway, we not only lost our equipment bundle on the drop, we didn't even find all the guys we jumped with."

"I was the jumpmaster and the only officer in that Pathfinder group. There was a crew chief sitting back with us but I don't think I had anything to do with the pilot or co-pilot. I just watched the terrain and the ready lights, and the crew chief released the equipment bundle when the time was right."

1st Sgt. William Lumsden of the HQ Co., 551st said, "Everything went wrong that possibly have gone wrong. They jumped us way off from where we were supposed to be, we lost our equipment bundles, and it was just cowboys and Indians, that sort of thing, for quite a while."

"There was some moonlight when I jumped and I could see that I was coming down right into an electrified rail yard. I was slipping desperately but there was no avoiding it and I came right down on the wires. When I hit, they must have been already shorted out because I could see electrical flashes and sparks flying, but it wasn't my doing. I fell from where I hit the wires and lay across the tracks, and had a pair of field glasses belted to the small of my back and they were squashed flat. I think another man hit the wires just before I did and he must have been the one who shorted everything out."

"Then the place became a complete maelstrom with people shouting and running about, shooting – a German came running up to me with his Schmeisser submachine gun and fired a burst right at me from ten feet away. I was still in my harness, lying on the ground. Then he turned and ran back and I got my .45 out, just by reflex, and shot him in the back. One round and down he went. I had carried it loaded on half-cock."

"Then I felt blood on my arm, one of his shots had gone through my left elbow. When I took off my reserve, there were four holes where his other shots had gone in, But none coming out. My reserve saved me. Then we got our selves together and moved out taking pieces of our parachutes with us for warmth when we slept."

T/5 Wendell E. Morrison of the HQ Co., 551st was the man reported by Sgt. Lumsden as having landed on the electrical lines causing the short just before he landed.

Pvt. Filipczak of the 517th recalls, "We unloaded on the apron in close proximity to the aircraft, and started to get ready. This really turned out to be one hell of a problem. After putting on our chute and reserve chute we then had to strap on our panels and in my case battery pack which weighed at least thirty pounds. This battery went under my reserve chute just below my knees. We could barely walk the fifteen or so steps to the aircraft. Air Corps people were there and lifted each of us into the plane."

"Our aircraft took some evasive maneuvers during flight to conceal our flight course. We were told jump time would be about 3:30 a.m. and at an altitude of 600 to 700 feet. We got the order to stand up, hook up, and good luck wishes from the Lieutenant. Most of my preceding thirteen jumps were between 600 to 1200 feet and you have an idea about time to ground impact. After leaving the aircraft I prepared myself at least three times for impact. The descent time was much longer than any of my previous jumps. I would guess it was at least 2500 feet. When I hit ground it was like a sack of shit. I got my equipment off, rifle out of the bag and listened for troopers. We had a password, which I softly called out. About fifteen to twenty minutes later I made contact with another trooper from my group. It was quite obvious that dropping from so high an altitude it separated us all over the place. We heard some small arms fire off on the distance and started in that direction. As daybreak started, we ran into three more troopers. We never heard or saw any aircraft in our vicinity. Later that afternoon we came across British glider troops. They took an enormous casualty count, not from the enemy, but from poles in the fields that were glider traps. Their large plywood gliders just splintered into pieces. It was tragic to see. It took us a day and a half to finally re-unite with our outfit. My buddies assumed I was dead, but happily I surprised them. By the way when morning broke, we threw the panels away, busted the battery, none of us had the radio".

"Although our pathfinder mission operation did not succeed, over-all our invasion into Southern France did."

Sgt. Jack Burns of the 517th was shot as he struggled to get out of his chute. But he recovered quickly, whipped out his .45 and shot the German in the head.

517th pathfinder Pvt. Joe Gavin, landed in a German position and was promptly captured while in his harness. He was rushed to a German Army command post, where a German Intelligence officer questioned him, demanding to know details of the airborne landings. For the next few hours, Gavin insisted that the operation had been launched from Brooklyn, N.Y. (two days later, seaborne forces would rescue him.).

509th Parachute Infantry Battalion

Drop Zone 'C'

1 Lt. Dan A Deleo	Team Leader	
Pvt. Vincent Klubster		
Pvt. Charles McDonald	*	Eureka Operator
Pvt. John Devanie	*	
Pvt. Charles Petty	B*	
Armstad		
Baum		
Culture		
Houghton		
Sgt. Steve Justice	KIA	
Pvt. Warren McGee		
Sweetitz	KIA	
Trzesckowski		
Pvt. Roland Rondeau		
Saiz		
1Sgt. James Prettyman	was assigned to the team in an administrative capacity	
Sgt. Manuel Serrano	Stowaway	

551st Parachute Infantry Battalion

Drop Zone 'O'

Lt. Russell S. Fuller	A	Team Leader
T/Sgt. 'Duke' Spletzer		
Pvt. Paul V. Balclavage	A	
Daniel J. Donovan	A	
Pvt. Roger p. Carqueville	HQ	
Carter		
Sgt. Hugh C. Roberts	B	
1Sgt. William W. Lumsden	HQ	
Pvt. Gerna W. Sizemore	A	
Pvt. William T. Crutsinger		
Francis M. McManus, Jr	C	MIA
Brown		
Lt. Hines		
Cpt. Tims Quinn	C	Co. Commander
1 Lt. Fank C. Serio	C	
1 Lt. John Milton hill	HQ	Co. Executive Officer
T/5 Wendall E. Morrison	HQ	KIA on drop

517th Parachute Infantry Regiment

Drop Zone 'A'

Sgt. Jack Burns	C	
Pvt. Joseph Gavin	C	
Sgt. Richard Robb	H	
Pvt. Buel E. Putnam	HQ 2 Bn. S-2 * Eureka Operator	
1 Lt. Robert B. Fuller	H	
Cpl. James Kitchen	G	
Pvt. Henry Filpczak		
Pfc. Henry A. Ciner	Regt./HQ	KIA 15 Aug. 1944 Near LaMuy

HOLLAND: 82nd Airborne - September 17, 1944

Due to the fact that Operation Market Garden was to take place during daylight hours it was decide that pathfinder personnel should be pin-pointed upon the drop zones preceding the main effort with only enough time to set into operation their navigational aides and place panel markings.

Even though the operation was to be a daylight drop, navigational aids would be used to ensure identification of routes and drop zones. Eureka beacons and compass beacons were to be set up at Troop Carrier Wing assembly points and departure points on the English coast. Marker boats with Eurekas and green holophane lights sending code letters were midway across the North Sea serving as reference points. Along the southern route aircraft would fly over a white panel T and yellow smoke five thousand yards before they would reach enemy lines after turning at the initial point near Gheel.

The final decision was that two teams, each consisting of one officer and eleven enlisted men be committed on DZ 'O', twenty-five minutes prior to the arrival of the main effort on that DZ. Elements to jump upon DZ 'N' and DZ 'T' were to fly over DZ 'O', guide upon navigational and visual aids, and continue to their respective DZs. These serials were to arrive in this order: Element for DZ 'N' at 1300, for DZ 'O' at 1310, and for DZ 'T' at 1328. Pathfinder drop-time was set for 1245.

In the first serial containing the 505th Parachute Infantry, the lead plane was to carry pathfinder personnel of that regiment, their mission to mark DZ 'N' for the remaining serials and subsequent resupply drops.

Pathfinder personnel of the 325th Glider Infantry jumped with the 508th Parachute Infantry on DZ 'T' to mark that LZ for glider landings.

All serials flying to all drop zones were dependent upon navigational aides established by pathfinders on DZ 'O'.

All officers and enlisted men had previous combat experience but had not participated in a combat pathfinder drop prior to Operation Market. Preparation and briefing were in conjunction with 101st Airborne pathfinders personnel, were conducted at the IX TCC Pathfinder Group War Room. Pilot-Jumpmaster conferences were as soon as DZs were assigned and pinpoints picked by Jumpmasters and Pilot-Navigator Teams. Regimental and Division Field Orders were studied in conjunction with maps for the operation. Each officer and NCO was issued a 1/25,000 scale map of the DZ area. All personnel received copies of 1/100,000 maps of area of operations. No maps were marked. Enlisted personnel were briefed twenty-four hours prior to the take-off. All personnel of the base were restricted from receipt of first orders until return of aircraft from the mission.

Air Corps-Airborne teams had been working together as such for approximately five months. Utmost confidence and coordination had been established. At all times the Air Corps pathfinder teams showed great willingness to cooperate with any suggestion presented by the Airborne troops.

Rations, ammunition, smoke, panels, etc., had been pre-drawn and were stored in the area several weeks prior to assignment of the mission. Equipment and uniforms for the pathfinders of the 82nd Airborne was the following according to 1st Lt. G. Wilfred Jaubert's after action report dated 30 Nov. 1944:

Equipment

Thompson submachine guns and M-1 rifles were weapons carried, each team supplied with six of each, All men carried pistols, Cal. .45, automatic in addition to their primary weapons.

Three D-ration bars and three K-rations were carried by each man.

Two hundred rounds of ammunition were supplied to each rifleman. Men armed with Thompsons with 210 rounds of ammunition.

All men carried trench knives and entrenching tools. First aid equipment was as follows:

6 ea, Packets, Sulfanilimide
1 ea, Packet, Prcht First-Aid
1 ea, Packet, First-Aid
1 ea, bottle, Halizone tablets

Two grenades, fragmentation and two grenades, smoke were carried by each man. Eight grenades, Gammon were divided among the personnel of the stick.

Due to the bulk of radar equipment some men requested permission to jump without reserve parachutes. Permission was granted but reserves were carried in the aircraft for every man.

Uniforms

Two-piece cotton jump suits were worn as outer garment with woolen sweater underneath. Woolen O.D. shirts and trousers were worn underneath the jump suits for warmth.

Caps, wool knit, with the visor removed, were worn under helmets.

Navigational Aids

DZ/LZ	Eureka Beacon	M/F Beacon	Panels	Smoke Color	Unit
DZ 'O'	code O	Freq 1495	Yellow O	Violet	82nd Pathfinders
DZ 'N'					82nd Pathfinders
DZ 'T'					82nd Pathfinders
DZ 'A'	code N	Freq 1425	Red A	Green	101st Pathfinders
DZ 'B'	code B	Freq 1525	White B	Red	101st Pathfinders
DZ 'C'	code B	Freq 1525	Yellow B	Violet	101st Pathfinders
LZ 'W'	code W	Freq 1525	White W	Red	101st Pathfinders
LZ 'N'	code N	Freq 1688	White N	Green	82nd Pathfinders
LZ 'T'	code N		Red T	Red	82nd Pathfinders

Aircraft heading for DZ/LZ 'N' and DZ/LZ 'T' would receive signals from DZ 'O'.

The final pathfinder briefing for aircrews and paratroops was held at 0830 on September 17, 1944 and immediately following all personnel proceeded to their assigned aircraft.

Team '1' composed of personnel from the 504th Prcht. Inf., commanded by 1st Lt. G.W. Jaubert, was assigned to aircraft #163. (1st Lt. E. Wood, pilot)

Team '2' composed of personnel from the 504th Prcht. Inf., commanded by 1st Lt. Donald Carlock, was assigned to aircraft #706. (1st Lt. McIntosh, pilot)

Mission of teams '1' and '2' was to drop upon and mark DZ 'O' for the main effort plus providing a check point for serials dropping on DZs 'N' and 'T', said serials to fly over DZ 'O' and using the radar navigational aides and panel markings for check points, continue on to their own DZs.

Pathfinder personnel were to drop on DZ 'O' fifteen minutes prior to the first serials and twenty-five minutes before their own main effort.

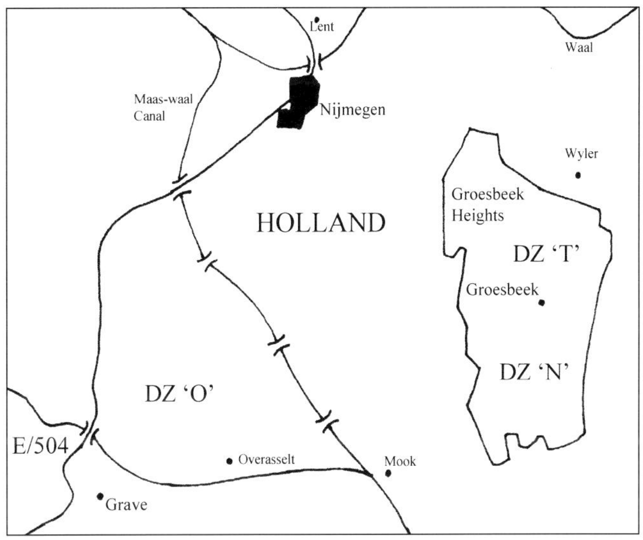

82nd Airborne Division drop zones 'N', 'O', and 'T' near Nijmegen, Holland.

After the 0830 briefings of aircraft crews and paratroopers the pathfinder teams took off at 1025 from Chalgrove Airdrome, circled, and followed a course generally east to the coast of France. Flying to the base of the British spearhead the ships turned north toward enemy held territory and upon crossing the plainly marked front lines speeded to 180 mph. Orange smoke was observed marking boundaries of friendly territory.

Friendly fighter escorts, in the form of P-47s, were abundant, giving the two ships all around cover. Enemy anti-aircraft fire encountered the enemy gun positions. A flak tower and flak wagon at Grave brought very heavy fire to bear upon the pathfinder personnel as they descended until fighters neutralized them. Immediately before dropping upon the DZ the P-47s was observed strafing the area heavily, completely disorganizing the enemy thereabouts.

The pathfinder drop was affected at exactly 1245, as planned, and pinpointed upon the exact predetermined spot. Pilots slowed their ships to the lowest speed possible in order to give the pathfinder teams as little dispersion as was possible. Aircraft did not fly abreast but, with #163 in lead, flew over the DZ with #706 on the right wing. As the jumpmaster of the latter ship observed the first chute leave the lead aircraft, he jumped his own team. In this manner the team landed side by side on the drop zone. Jump height was 450 feet.

Upon assembly, which was immediate due to the excellent drop given by the pilots, the panel 'T' was put into position and all smoke dropped at the end of the leg. Due to the scarcity of smoke, it was decided that the senior team leader would use the grenades at his discretion.

No immediate enemy resistance was encountered and Team '1' experienced no difficulty in setting into operation their navigational sides. The panel markings and navigational aides were all in place within three minutes. Team '2' acted as local security since the other team suffered no casualties or enemy interference.

First serial of the element to jump upon DZ 'N' appeared at 1300. Twelve minutes later, at 1312, the first serial of the main effort arrived on DZ 'O'. The second and third serials arrived at 1315 and 1318 respectively. The main effort landed upon the drop zone in good order, receiving some anti-aircraft fire. There was no hesitation in assembly and, forty-five minutes after the last serial jumped, the entire field was cleared. At 1328 the first serial of the element to jump on DZ 'T' was observed flying over DZ 'O'.

Pathfinder personnel remained upon the drop zone until D plus seven, at which time they were relieved of their duties in that capacity. No casualties were suffered by pathfinder personnel up to that date.

S/Sgt. Ervin Kitchenmaster recalls, "One month before the Holland jump I had been assigned as a replacement to Co. C, 325th Glider Infantry Regiment, 82nd Airborne Division. Because of the heavy losses incurred in the glider landings on D-Day in Normandy, the 325th decided to form it's own 'Pathfinder Team'. In the next airborne mission, these 'Pathfinders' would jump ahead of the gliders and bring the Regiment in to the proper landing zone (LZ) with panel markings and radar. (New at the time) I was one of the thirty-six men from the regiment to volunteer for jump training to form this new Team."

"The first week of training was concentrated on the technique of jumping and how to handle yourself during the jump. The second week we made our five qualifying jumps and received our Parachute Jump Wings."

"As we resumed training with our company, rumors abounded of planed Airborne Operations. In early September, we Pathfinders were pulled from our units and assembled at an airfield staging area. We were located in a hangar with men of the 508th Parachute Regiment, which was attached to the 82nd for this operation. Briefed for our mission we learned that we would be part of the 1st Allied Airborne Army and our destination was the area near Groesbeek, Holland. We were each issued a small amount of 'invasion money'. This was Dutch Guilders printed and packed by the Allied Army. That night an American Indian trooper of the 508th built a small bonfire in our hangar and did a war dance around it."

"Sunday morning, September 17, 1944, our serial of C-47 'Dakotas' lifted off from England into beautiful sunshine and good weather. The Allied Airborne Army was in the air for the invasion of Holland, Operation Market-Garden. From horizon to horizon as far as the eye could see, the sky was full of planes. This armada was made up of the British 1st Airborne Division, the American 82nd and 101st Airborne Divisions and a Brigade of Polish Paratroopers."

"Our 325th Pathfinders were in two planes with eighteen men in each team. We lifted off about 10 a.m., each of us tense and lost in our own thoughts as we headed out over the North Sea. As we approached the Dutch coast, anti-aircraft fire started bursting around us. We could see the dark bursts and tracers through the open door on our plane. The doors had been removed in advance for convenience in jumping and to facilitate a quick exit if required in an emergency."

"As a Staff Sergeant I was one of the ranking NCOs in our plane. My mind was on our 'drop zone'. Would we be shot to pieces before we reached the ground? Our signal light came on. I took my position at one side of the open door and Lt. Harry Teras moved to the other side. Two German fighter planes zoomed past our plane so close the black cross was clearly visible on their fuselage. Bursting anti-aircraft shell and small arms fire rattled all through the plane. I was expecting to feel German machine gun bullets rip through my flesh at any time. We learned later that several men in the other pathfinder plane were wounded before reaching the drop zone and returned to England with the plane."

"The drop zone came up rapidly, the green light came on, Lt. Teras flipped the switch for equipment drop and out the door he went. I pushed out the door just a fraction of a second behind Teras and the others in our plane came out just as fast. Sgt. Edward Adams, another Company C man brought up the rear."

"We landed in a new growth of timber with heavy underbrush and pine trees. Visibility in this dense foliage was almost nil. I got clear of my parachute harness as quickly as possible, took concealment and called out the password ... 'Red and Charlie'. The response I got was small arms bullets cracking over my head. After waiting a few minutes, I started walking

Opposite
Top: This picture of 325th Glider Infantry men was taken before boarding a C-47 for Holland on Sept. 17, 1944. Pfc. Hirlemann is in front on his elbow, S/Sgt. Ervin Kitchenmaster on the right side, and a trooper by the name of Stacey is standing on the far right. The others are all unknown. *Courtesy of Ervin Kitchenmaster*

Bottom: Two unidentified pathfinders of the 325th Glider Infantry before the Holland invasion. *Courtesy of Ervin Kitchenmaster*

in the direction I thought would take me to the other men in my 'stick'."

"After a short walk I arrived at the edge of the woods, feeling very lonely. I saw a small house and walked to it. A Dutchman who lived there invited me in and gave me a drink of powdered milk. That tasted good for I had eaten nothing since breakfast at the airfield in England. Since it was near evening and not wanting to be ambushed by a German patrol I returned to the woods and found a place to stay for the night. In the distance I thought I could hear gunfire but I saw no American GIs and no civilians except the one old Dutchman."

"The next morning I started out of the woods and almost shot another trooper as we surprised each other in the dense underbrush. This man was searching for his light artillery unit as I was looking for my Pathfinders. It is possible that the hostile fire I met when I gave the password on landing came from this lost trooper."

"Now with a friend for company, we decided to set off for Nijmegen. My new friend said he knew where the was a German Army barracks with canned beef, champagne, and wine so we made that our first stop and feasted our fill. Two American GIs were there ahead of us, and on the same mission, to eat a good meal. This barracks had been ransacked by the 508th. There were a lot of deer hide duffel bags scattered around on the bunks. The next morning we made it into Nijmegen, getting a lift on a horse drawn Dutch farm wagon. We saw no American troops and no motorized vehicles along our route."

"As we approached the outskirts of Nijmegen we heard artillery firing, walking toward it and into my friends artillery unit. I bid him good-bye and started back on the road to Groesbeek. I saw no civilians along the route for they were hiding in their homes. As darkness fell on September 19th I found the 82nd Airborne Division Headquarters located in the Groesbeek Woods, Northwest of Groesbeek. At this headquarters I was told that the 325th's landing area had been changed to LZ 'O' and was given directions to find this area and my Pathfinder team."

"At dawn the next day I again started out to find my friends. On this trip I saw my first dead troopers. They had made the supreme sacrifice in a fire-fight at a small bridge over a canal. A glider pilot who had sought shelter in one of the windmills had been hit in the head by a shell fragment as he was sleeping. The fragment had penetrated the side of the windmill before hitting the pilot in the head."

"Walking along the road leading to the glider LZ I came to a small country bar. I noticed a man inside so I went in and presented my 'invasion guilders' for a glass of beer. The area outside was deserted and the bartender and I were the only ones present. I quickly drank my beer, for my mind was on the action yet to come when the gliders arrived."

"Now on the right road, I approached my unit and was sighted by Lt. Teras and Sgt. Adams, Both men came running to greet me, their excitement and elation was very evident. They told me they thought I had run into bade luck and gone to Airborne Heaven! They had not expected to see me again. It was a happy meeting for me too; I was again back with my friends, the pathfinders."

"Lt. Teras told me that upon landing and moving to the assigned glider LZ there appeared to be a lot of movement in a patch of nearby woods. An officer senior to Lt. Teras ordered him to take his pathfinders and clear the patch of woods. Teras moved his troops to good firing positions near the woods and opened fire. When no more movement could be seen in the woods, Lt. Teras moved in to investigate. There were several young German soldiers, one a very young captain, all dead. This was an unusual fire fight for the pathfinders received very little return fire. Perhaps the Germans wanted to surrender but this is unlikely since they were fighting on the border of their Fatherland."

"Because of bad weather, the gliders bringing the 325th Glider Infantry were delayed in England. During this time our pathfinder team was strafed twice by German fighters. One of our men was literally caught with pants down when he had stopped to defecate and a German plane came over strafing the area. Fortunately, no one was hit."

"We watched daily 'dog fights' in the air. One day I saw five American planes go down to three German. The German went into a steep dive, we expected to see him crash but he pulled out of the dive, his tail almost hitting the ground. A British officer standing near us said, 'That Jerry deserves to live after a piece of flying like that!' But, the Spitfires got back on his tail and we saw a spiral of smoke in the distance. We assume the Spitfire got his 'kill' that day."

"Our 'invasion money' was much appreciated as we waited for the weather to clear. A lady in a dairy farm accepted our money and sold us mashed potatoes and unsweetened applesauce. We were living high!"

"The weather cleared on the 23rd of September and we manned the signal panels and stood by with our smoke grenades to bring our 325th Regiment into the LZ. The 508th manned the radar sets and the Troop Carriers deposited the gliders on target. As the mass of gliders cut loose and maneuvered for a patch of open area on which to land there appeared to be total confusion but our men came pouring out. An over zealous B.A.R. team quickly fell into firing position and opened fired in our direction. The troops were very excited and did not recognize us at first. No one was hit but a bullet did go through the radar set."

"As the 325th Regiment moved to their assembly area, we pathfinders rejoined our units. Lt. Teras, Sgt. Adams, Pfc Jablonski, Cpl. Barker, Pfc Abeyta, and I returned to Company C, 1st Battalion."

S/Sgt Kitchenmaster would be seriously wounded days later near Mook, Holland and evacuated.

HOLLAND: 101st Airborne - September 17, 1944

For the Normandy campaign, the 101st Airborne Division had used eleven sticks of pathfinders to cover the three drop zones and one glider landing area.

Because the Holland jump was a daylight mission, the number of pathfinder teams was reduced to four, with one stick being assigned for each drop zone. The 501st Parachute Infantry Regiment had Drop Zone 'A' in the Eerda area, west of Veghel and Drop Zone 'A-1' just to the northwest of Veghel between the Aa River and the Zuid-Willems-Vaart Canal on the north side of the railroad track. The 502nd was assigned DZ 'B', which would put the regiment in close proximity to both best and St. Oedenrode. The 506th would land on DZ 'C'. Its southern boundary was the northern edge of the Zonsche Forest. The glider-landing zone extended beyond the boundaries of both DZs 'B' and 'C' and provided a huge area in which to land hundreds of CG-4A gliders.

In Normandy, the serials of troop-carrying planes had relied heavily on the Eureka-Rebecca radar sets and the 'T's formed with holophane lights angled in such a way that they could be seen only from the approaching aircraft.

For the Holland mission, the paratroopers relied on the radar sets to home in the planes from distance of twenty miles. Once the planes came into view, orange smoke bombs were set off to provide visual sightings. The pathfinders also laid out panels in the form of a large 'T' to further direct the incoming planes.

The soldier who packed all the parachutes for the pathfinder teams was T/5 Glenn Braddock. His recollections of the preparations after the Normandy campaign had been completed are as follows: "Shortly after the Normandy mission, after we had received our recuperation furloughs (during this time I was transferred from the Rigger Section of Service Company to the 502nd Regimental Headquarters Company) we were organized again and moved in to an air base outside of Oxford, England – Chalgrove Airbase, I believe."

"We received a new group of men to train as replacements; also, we were resupplied on equipment, some of which had just arrived from the States and required our own type of testing. The men we selected for the pathfinder training remained and the others went back to their original companies. We then continued more rigid sessions of renewed training."

In the days prior to the Holland jump the pathfinder teams were reduced to fourteen men. As the mission approached the teams were once again reduced to ten men each.

"On the 15th of September, some of our men were granted passes, I being one of the luckier ones, having a high time in Nottingham when (Thomas G.) 'Glider-Flaps' Walton caught up with me and said we were to report back to the base – that we were designated for possibly another mission."

"On the night of the 16th we were under quarters and area arrest. This time there were no barbed wire enclosures around us and our only guards were at the supply room and my parachute shed. (The MP's maintained a constant dog patrol on my parachute packing shed unless I was present and at work.) Lt. Robert Smith of the 377th Parachute Field Artillery was my parachute supply officer."

1st Lt. Gordon DeRamus, Jr., had been a mortar platoon officer in Normandy. He found himself in charge of one of the four pathfinder teams. He listed the direction equipment carried by the teams as: "Two Eureka sets, one CRN-4, seven green lights, seven orange panels, seven white panels, and five cases of orange smoke grenades."

There was a mission but the pathfinders didn't know where they were going. T/5 Glenn Braddock continued his narrative: "We went to breakfast more or less as a group and when we returned, received orders to prepare for combat; supplies and chutes were issued and much excitement prevailed. Where were we going? Nobody knew, but we were told we'd receive our flight plans and orders of action at the planes."

"There really hadn't been time for rehearsals. Three earlier missions had been cancelled. The stay at the marshaling area for the regiments and battalions had been two days duration."

After the 0830 briefings of aircraft crews and paratroops the pathfinders of the 82nd took off from Chalgrove airfield at 1025 followed by two pair from the 101st at ten minute intervals on September 17, 1944. They had a P-47 fighter escort from the 78th Fighter Group over the Channel but none over the Continent.

The two serials of two planes each landfall together over the Belgian coast. The rear pair (headed for DZs 'B' and 'C') circled to re-establish its time interval while the lead pair flew on toward DZs 'A' and 'A-1'. Both pair sighting the orange smock set out near Gheel to mark the front, and both ran into heavy fire over the German lines. Evasive action was forbidden. All the pilots could do was speed their lumbering lanes to 180 miles per hour or alter the altitude on approach. The drop zones were now twenty-five miles away.

Near Ratie, one of the pair bound for Veghel area (DZ 'A-1') was hit in the left engine and wing tank by 20mm anti-aircraft fire and crashed in flames. The ill-fated plane, #42-100981 nicknamed "Chevelet" belonged to the 9th Troop Carrier Pathfinder Group. It was piloted by 1st Lt. Eugene Shauvin.

1st Lt. Bob Centers, flying one of the other planes, reported: "Lt. Shauvin flew in the second position on our right wing and stayed with us till about 1230 hours at about 1400 feet when we started our run. We had just passed the front line when we were shot at by very accurate anti-aircraft gunners. As we had lots to do in controlling our plane, we did not check on Lt. Shauvin's plane. When it was quiet, we did not see any plane in the far surroundings."

T/5 Glenn Braddock was on board the plane piloted by Lt. Robert Centers and the team assigned to mark DZ 'A'. Braddock wrote: "I was jumping last as clean-up man in Lt. Smith's plane. I had drawn straws with another trooper (Cpl. Roy L.) Stephens and had lost so I would be in the same plane with Sgt. John O'Shaughnesssey, who was jumping directly behind the lieutenant."

"Lt. Charles Faith (Stephens was in his stick) and his pathfinders were in the second 501st plane. Although I was a 502nd man, I went in with the 501st team. We were all trained in the duties required of pathfinders, regardless of which company or regiment we came from and any man could replace any position on the team."

"We were joking above the roar of the engines on the plane to our left and the Canadian fighter escort that accomplished us. Lt. Faith's plane was flying just to the left and a little behind and below us. A voice over the intercom said, 'Don't you love me anymore?' and damn if the pilot of the second plane didn't fly and put his wing tip right in the door of our plane – Christ! I thought we would crash. The pilot barely dropped off and as I was watching the other plane, I heard a loud explosions and rattle like heavy hail on the roof. Lt. Faith's plane started smoking and the left front end went down with smoke spewing out behind."

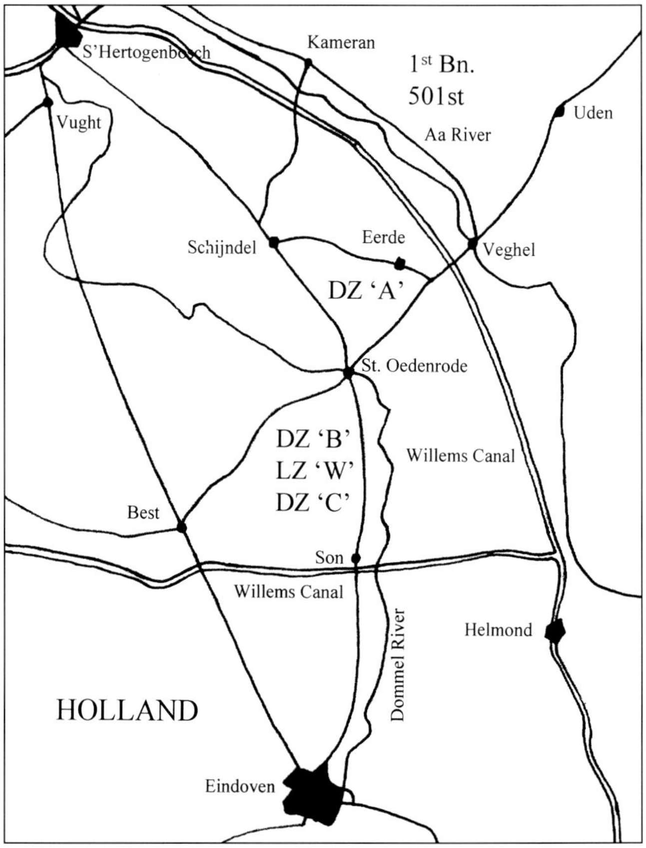

101st Airborne Division drop zones 'A', 'B', and 'C' and LZ 'W' north of Eindoven, Holland.

"The Canadian escort – up to this time playing 'ring around the rosie' with us – seemed to have disappeared and, as I looked out the window of our plane, a huge hole appeared just off the leading edge of the wing and about six feet back. I quit looking out that window as I was too damned busy thinking when that next slug was coming up through the bottom of the plane between me and the navigator's compartment and hitting me in the butt – holes were coming through the bottom and going out through the roof with little streamers of fire attached to some of them – TRACERS!!! Up to his this time the navigator's door had been open but when the barrage started it was closed."

"Then we heard the heavy, sharp whine of diving planes – 'Flak tower to the left and firing at us', someone shouted. The diving aircraft screamed past us and I saw it firing tracers at the top of the tower and then a fiery jettison of what appeared to be a rocket – the lower went up in dust and smoke – boy! were we relieved. There was no more flak but I knew we had lost one of our planes and the entire pathfinder stick going in to the 501st DZ with us. Bastards!"

Four crew members and four pathfinders, including Cpl. Roy L. Stephens, died in that crash. The other six pathfinders successfully cleared the aircraft. The pilot, Lt. Shauvin, badly injured, and five pathfinders were taken prisoner. Lt. Charles Faith evaded capture and was found by the Belgian underground, hiding from the enemy until they retreated from the area and then sent back to England.

Fortunately, the surviving aircraft flew safely and accurately to Veghel, sighted the railway which bounded the zone on the north, turned parallel to the tracks and made its run right over the zone. At 1247 hours, it dropped its troops on DZ 'A' from standard altitude, at minimum speed. The paratroops met no resistance and were able to put the Eureka in operation in a minute and to lay out the panels in two-and-a-half minutes. They had trouble with the radio antenna but had that set working within five minutes. The smoke signals were not set off until the main serials were in sighted.

T/5 Glenn Braddock continues his story: "We had slipped down to low-level flying when the firing started and Lt. Smith called back, 'Stand up, hook up and check equipment!' which we did, hurriedly. We were ready to jump on a second order if we were lucky enough to clear the plane."

"After the flak tower was knocked out, we flew low for a short period of time, maybe five minutes, and someone said, 'Red light, recheck hookup and equipment.'"

"The plane started a slight climb and banked to the left sharply. In looking out of the window, I could see the end of a canal and what appeared to be a series of cross or intermingled roads. In the middle of this was an old man and a little girl holding his hand and waving at us. The plane straightened out, leveled off and the green light came on. I came down through the top of a barbed wire fence which tumbled me rather roughly on the soft dirt."

There were anxious moments on Drop Zone 'A'. Having jumped as the last man in the stick, T/5 Braddock had this recollection: "After struggling out of my harness and still trying to clear my head from that tumble I got after hitting the barbed wire fencing, I tried to line up just where the rest of the stick had landed on the other side of the trees."

"'They're over here!' I heard Ernest Stene yell. He added, 'Hold it, there's someone spotted us and coming down the road toward us.'"

"I waited until a soldier in a kind of bluish uniform was right across the road from me – a distance of about fifteen yards. I called out 'Halt!' the safety was off on my Thompson sub and I knew that one bad move would have been his last. Although he was armed with a pistol, he made no effort to draw it, and said 'Take me to your commandment.' I said, 'Ah, you speak

Pathfinders of the 501st Para. Inf. Regt., 101st Abn. Div. pose in front of their C-47 prior to a training jump in early September 1944 before the teams were reduced to ten men. This team was assigned to mark DZ 'A-1' northwest of Veghel, which was shot down. Back row left to right: Lt. Charles Faith, Pvt. George Sarles, Pvt. Ernest Robinson, Pvt. Spencer Everly. Pvt. Michael Rufar, Pvt. Alvin Haux, Green, Cpl. Roy L. Stephens. Front row: Quin, Pvt. Lester Hunt, Cpl. Delbert Brazzle, T/5 Richard Beaver, Pvt Francis Rocca, Cary. *Courtesy of Mark Bando*

Pathfinders of the 501st and 502nd Para. Inf. Regt., 101st Abn. Div. pose in front of their plane prior to departure for a training jump in early September 1944 once again before the team was reduced to ten men. Left to right: Pvt. John Zamankos, T/5 Tom Walton, T/5 Glen Braddock, Pfc. John Kleifelder, Pvt. Raymond Smith, Sgt. John O'Shaughnessey, Cpt. Frank Brown, Pvt. Buford Williams, Pfc. Delbert Jones, Cpl. Murphy, Pfc. Fred Wilhelm, Pfc. William B. Mench, John Hopke, Pfc. William Casey. *Courtesy of George Koskimaki*

English.' He nodded and said 'Yes' and raised his hand above his shoulders and up both sides of the ditches men in different attire rose up, each armed with a weapon. I kept my Thompson sub machine gun trained on him and said, 'Tell your men not to move or I'll kill you!' Meanwhile, I heard someone say, 'Where in hell is Braddock with the rest of the equipment?'"

"'Stene – Stene - Come over here!' I yelled. 'Come over here quick!' Stene came over on the double and I quickly explained – 'This soldier claims to be a Dutch underground officer but as far as I am concerned he is still enemy.'"

"'Take my equipment, and with him in front of you, take him to Lt. Robert Smith. If he makes a bad move, kill him. If I hear a shot I'll start shooting likewise. If you hear a shot from this direction – let the rest of the stick know someone is with you or they might start shooting at you.'"

"'I will stay here and act as security for the rest of the team so they can take whatever precautions are necessary.'"

"'Have you heard and understood what we have just been talking about?' I asked the officer and he replied that he did. 'OK then, instruct your men to stay as they are until I walk out to the middle of the road.'"

"He spoke to them in Dutch and Stene ushered him to the rest of the stick and Lt. Smith."

"The others were busy getting the Eureka in operation and had set out the panels. The smoke grenades were ready to be exploded just as soon as the planes came into view."

"There were some very tense and nervous moments from the time I first saw the underground men until after our troops started dropping from the skies. The Dutch never made a move to take their weapons off their shoulders where they were slung and when the first parachutes opened and started drifting earthward they cheered and gave lights claps with their hands. I was still very nervous and doubtful until I saw one of our troopers coming around a bend in the road and I stepped out in the middle of the road to wave him on. It was Lt. Smith and the underground officer already shaking hands with the point echelon of parachutists from the 501st going toward Veghel."

The pair of planes slated for DZs 'B' and 'C' dropped their teams side by side with pinpoint accuracy at 1254. They had slowed to less than ninety miles per hour for the jump, and the men landed so close together that no assembly was necessary. The Eureka was in operation in less than a minute, and the panels and radio were ready within four minutes. Although a few enemy troops were in the vicinity, they were readily disposed of without affecting the pathfinder's work.

1st Lt. Gordon DeRamus provided a brief description of his landings on Drop Zone 'C'. "After a very uneventful flight (the last two planes were not a in the vicinity when Lt. Shauvin's plane was shot down), we were dropped at 600 feet over the DZ near Son. There was no opposition on the field."

Serving as medic for the pathfinder teams, Pvt. Raymond Smith noted: "Before my feet touched the ground, I could see a German soldier fleeing the drop zone on a motorcycle. There were no other enemy soldiers near our area at Son."

"We got there about thirty minutes ahead of the main body of troops." Added Lt. DeRamus. "We were met by several Dutch underground boys who told us of locations of Krauts near the DZ. We set up our equipment and formed protection around it."

The Dutch underground also had been preparing for the invasion by the Allies.

Johannes J, van Gorkum was twenty-three years old at the time of the airborne operation in Holland. During the war years, he was a member of the LKP group of St. Oedenrode under the command of Sjef De Groot. Since September of 1943, they had worked together with the Theo van Schijndel, M. Boere, M. Bouwman and M. Van Aken, all from the St. Oedenrode area. The last four had been captured and executed by the Germans during the past year.

Describing his part in the airborne landings, van Gorkum related: "My code name was 'Joe' and together with Piet J. Jeuke in the underground HQ in Nijmegen, orders came from Sjef De Groot to go to the Zonsche heath fields. Sjef De Groot and its colleagues would go to a field between Schijndel and St. Oedenrode (501st DZ 'A')."

"Our instructions were to be alert and ready to help and provide information, if necessary. Nothing was mentioned to us of a landing and nobody knew what was going on. As we rode our bicycles toward the fields, we heard the sound of planes. We saw a German plane pursued by an English fighter. These planes were flying very low and making a lot of noise. We could clearly see their markings."

"After that a scouting plane (pathfinders) came and several parachutists came down. My colleague, who was riding up front, pedaled his bike so fast I was unable to keep up with him as he rode toward the landing place. I left by bike at farmer Sanders and started running toward the paratroopers. When I was within thirty meters one of them shouted, 'Hands-up!! I quickly put my hands up as weapons were pointed at me. At this time I wished I could go back as I was scared. Piet, in the meantime, had informed them who we were."

Pvt. Raymond Smith, who had suffered a broken ankle on the Normandy pathfinder jump, described some of the actions of the team members: "The mission of the pathfinder team was to mark the drop zone with four foot by eight foot identifying panels placed in a 'T' shape and to guide the planes in with the Eureka radar set."

Pfc. Fred Wilhelm, a member of the same stick, said: "The Air Force assured us that nothing would move (against us) on the field. My job was to lay out the panels in the form of a 'T' and to use the orange smoke bombs."

No individual German soldiers threatened their presence. However, this didn't prevent enemy soldiers from firing light artillery and mortars at the men from a distance. Some time later, mortar shells began to land on the Son DZ.

Pfc. Wilhelm added, "After we had set up our navigation aids, Zamanakos, Smith, and I were standing together talking, as we were good buddies from way back. A shell hit near us and Zamanakos was struck in the chest."

"I was hit about a half hour after landing and setting up panels – it was just before the arrival of the planes," said Cpl. John Zamanakos. "I was the radar operator."

Zamanakos mission ended abruptly. He said, "Medic Ray Smith patched me up and I was treated at a civilian hospital in Don." This was the end of the Holland campaign for Zamanakos.

From his vantage point on Drop Zone 'C', Lt. DeRamus had this to add: "The main body of troops came in around thirty minutes later, and its seems as though the Krauts must have known something because I saw around seventeen C-47s shot down on the fields around us."

Johannes van Gorkum continued his assistance at the Son drop zone. He added: "The landing went really well but from the direction of Best, light German cannons were shooting at the planes. Suddenly, I noticed an orange parachute. I rushed toward the parachutist and he spoke to me in perfect Dutch. He said he was a radioman and asked for directions to Son. Together we went to a captain who had all his men assembled. I told him how many German soldiers were in Best and Son. The captain was heading in another direction and the information did not pertain to him. He suggested I give that information to others. We wished him success and together with the radioman, we started toward Son. Near the farm of H. van Gervern, we met two old Jewish people that I helped to hide on the farm. They gave me a big hug and thanked me for what I had done for them. Then I sent the radio man to Son and never heard from him again."

Lt. DeRamus continued: "The next day we set up panels and radio equipment for resupply. We stayed there for a couple days, directing other serials until the missions were completed and then moved north to regimental headquarters of the 502nd where I was assigned as 1st Battalion mortar platoon leader."

Commenting on his part in later pathfinder actions, Raymond Smith wrote: "The next two or three days, following the invasion of the 17th of September, brought very sad memories for me. We pathfinders continued the procedure of marking drop zones for glider troops and supplies but the German Air Force still had plenty of fighting planes to shoot down our transport planes and I witnessed dozens of dog fights between Allied and German pilots. In France we didn't encounter this kind of action. We lost planes and gliders to anti-aircraft artillery."

Even though 1st Battalion of the 501st Regiment wasn't directed to the proper drop zone, forty-two planes of the forty-five plane serial managed to land its troopers in a very compact pattern despite the fact that it mint a double-time march of three miles from the Heeswijk-Dinter castle area near Kameran. Opposition was almost non-existent and the local residents provided much help.

The 101st pathfinders remained on the DZ for a week performing their pathfinder mission guiding in resupply drops and glider landings.

502nd Parachute Infantry Regiment, 101st Airborne Division

Drop Zone 'A'

Left to right

Pvt. John Zamanikos	HQ *	
T/5 Tom Walton	*	
T/5 Glen Braddock	*	
Pfc. John D. Kleinfelder	C *	
Pvt. Raymond Smith		Medic
Sgt. John O'Shaughnessy	B/501st *	
Cpt. Frank Brown	HQ *	Team Leader
Pfc. Buford R. Williams	*	
Pfc. Delbert A. Jones	B *	
Cpl. John M. Murphy	HQ/ 377 PFA *	
Pfc. Fred A. Wilhelm	*	
Pfc. William B. Mench	D *	
Pfc. John Hopke		
Pfc. William G. Casey	G *	
1 Lt. Robert G. Smith	HQ/377 PFA *	Not in picture
Lt. Robert Centers		Air Crew - Pilot

501st/502nd Parachute Infantry Regiment, 101st Airborne Division

Drop Zone 'A-1'

1 Lt. Charles M. Faith	HQ/501 *	Team Leader Evaded capture
Cpl. Roy L. Stephens		Killed in crash 17 Sept. 1944
Pvt. Michael Rofer	I/501 *	Killed in crash 17 Sept. 1944
Pvt. George L. Sarlas	3/501 *	Killed in crash 17 Sept. 1944
Cpl. Delbert S. Brazzle	A/501 *	Killed in crash 17 Sept. 1944
Pvt. Alvin Haux	HQ 3/501*	
T/5 Donald N. Green	A/377 PFA *	
Steavens		
T/5 Jerrold J.Quin	B/377 PFA	
Pvt. Lester Hunt	HQ/501*	
T/5 Richard H. Beaver	2/501*	
Pvt. Francis A. Rocca	C/502 *	
PFC Donald E. Cary	502	Killed in crash 17 Sept. 1944
Pvt. Ernest A. Robinson	3/501 *	
Pvt. Spencer E. Everly	I/501 *	
1 Lt. Eugene Shauvin		Air Crew- Pilot
2 Lt. John F. Richards	Navigator	Killed in crash 17 Sept. 1944

Others unknown

This is the team that was shot down south of Eindhoven. The plane was nicknamed 'Chevelet'. Four crewmen and four pathfinders were killed in the crash and the pilot was severely injured. One pathfinder evaded and five other pathfinders were taken prisoner.

506th Parachute Infantry Regiment, 101st Airborne Division

Drop Zone 'C'

1 Lt. Gordon DeRamus	*
1 Lt. Robert S. Dickson	S-2

(Others unknown)

BASTOGNE - December 22, 1944

On December 22, 1944, at 1130 hours, Lt.Col. John W. Oberdorf, head of Troop Carrier Command A-3, telephoned Col. Crouch at Chalgrove to prepare for an "immediate" two-plane pathfinder mission. One hour later, Maj. Lightfoot called with further orders committing the Pathfinder Group to a forty aircraft paradrop resupply mission to Bastogne, originating at Membury. A few minutes later the pathfinders of the 101st Airborne Division were alerted for a two-stick pathfinder mission by orders from Lt.Col. James T. Blair, Executive Officer, IX Troop Carrier Command Pathfinder Group. (Airborne Pathfinders participating in this operation were not permanently assigned to the IX TCC Pathfinder Group, but were on temporary duty to the while attending school for two weeks. It was merely a coincidence that sufficient Airborne Pathfinders to accomplish the mission were available at this base at the time of the mission was received.).

Their mission was to parachute in around Bastogne, Belgium where the 101st Airborne was surrounded by the Germans in order to coordinate resupply drops. The IX Troop Carrier Command gave the resupply mission the name, Operation "Kangaroo." The division was to commit one stick (one officer and nine enlisted men) to mark the drop zone.

Recognizing the serious lack of current battle maps, Col. Crouch decided to head to IX Troop Carrier Command Headquarters at Grantham, a half-hour's drive by jeep, to get the latest and firsthand instructions. He left Lt. Col. Blair and the XVIII Corps (Airborne) pathfinder officer, Capt. Frank Brown, to organize the two-plane pathfinder mission until he returned. He intended to fly the lead pathfinder plane to Bastogne. However, his initial plans were subverted.

Due to the fact that the DZ was known to be surrounded by the Germans and considering the effect of small area fire on the C-47 type aircraft at jump altitude (400-600 feet) the XO, IX TCC Pathfinder Group ND the XVII Corps (Airborne) Pathfinder Officer felt that two identical teams should be committed. A telephone (scrambler) request to commit two teams was approved by the IX Troop Carrier Command.

Coordinates of the DZ with as much intelligence data as was available was telephoned (scrambled) to the IX TCC Pathfinder Group at 1130 hours with instructions to have personnel airborne at 1400 hours to facilitate checking of teams and equipment on the ground during daylight hours.

The pathfinders were equipped with weapons and combat equipment by the S-3. Smoke and panels had been pre drawn and were available in the XVIII Corps supply room. Radar

Left to right: Lt. Schrable D. Williams, Cpl. John Dewey (nearly covered), Sgt. Jake McNiece, Pvt. Charles Partlow, Pvt. Lochman M. Tillman, Pfc. Carl L. Fenstermaker, and Pfc. Jack Agnew on the bricks signaling incoming aircraft in Bastogne on 23 December 1944. *Courtesy of 101st Airborne Division Association*

equipment was to be set up and checked. Due to limited time all enlisted personnel of the two teams were dispatched to the dispersal areas to load at 1330 hours. Officer jumpmasters reported to Group Operations for Pilot-Jumpmaster briefing at this time.

The two teams of pathfinders would drop with the following equipment:

Six Eureka (AN/PPN-1A) sets
Three CRN-4's
Fourteen Halophane Lights
Fourteen AP 50's (red fluorescent)
Twenty AP 30's (white)
Six cases of smoke grenades

Intelligence reports relative to enemy and friendly situations on the ground indicated the situation in the area was fluid and a close map reconnaissance of the DZ was impossible due to a lack of large scale (1:25,000) maps of the area. The pathfinders were furnished with (1:100,000) maps of the area. At the time limit from receipt of necessary information to take off (thirty minutes) did not allow time for proper briefing of course and preparation for emergency operations under the circumstances. Combined Air Corps and pathfinder teams took off at 1452 hours.

Commanding Officer, IX TCC Pathfinder Group returned to his headquarters at 1455 hours and checked prior preparations made in his absence. After checking weather and sunset time he radioed the Flight Leader to return to base. Message was confirmed and the flight returned to base

During the night of 22 December all available information in reference to the operation was obtained. Maps (1:50,000) were furnished to the pathfinders, a final briefing was given, and the flight took off as scheduled at 0645 hours on December 23.

Since up to the minute intelligence reports were unobtainable it was decided to drop one stick and wait for a predetermined signal (orange smoke grenade) prior to dropping the second stick. This was in order to definitely determine if the pathfinders were in friendly territory.

From daylight on December 23, all guards stood alert for the first appearance of the C-47s. At 0935 hours a military policeman on guard duty at the entrance to the 101st Airborne Division command post in Bastogne carried word to Col. Kohls that several large planes were circling the area.

A few minutes later the first plane of pathfinders was dropped by Lt.Col. Joel L. Crouch, from C-47 #993. 1st Lt. Schrable Williams and his team landed in the area where the 2nd Battalion of Col. Harper's 327th Glider Infantry was deployed. This was the exact spot agreed upon by the pilot and jumpmaster. Orange smoke and a signal from their Eureka beacon indicated they were in friendly territory. The second team and bundles were dropped at the same location by 1st Lt. Lionel E. Wood flying C-47 #681, consisted of 1st Lt. Gordon O. Rothwell's team.

At 0730 hours on December 22 the task of recovering the supplies was given to Maj. William H. Butler, the S-4 for the 506th Parachute Infantry. He got vehicles and crews alerted and ready, went to the drop zone, put out the signal panel to guide the planes, and then waited. When the mission was delayed the panels were taken up and the men went back to their post.

After arriving Lt. Rothwell telephoned Col. Kohls that the supply planes would be arriving in about ninety minutes. Col. Kohls told him how to get to the drop zone and where to put the radar set. Again the regimental supply men were alerted for the drop and Maj. Butler displayed the orange signal panels in the form of a "T".

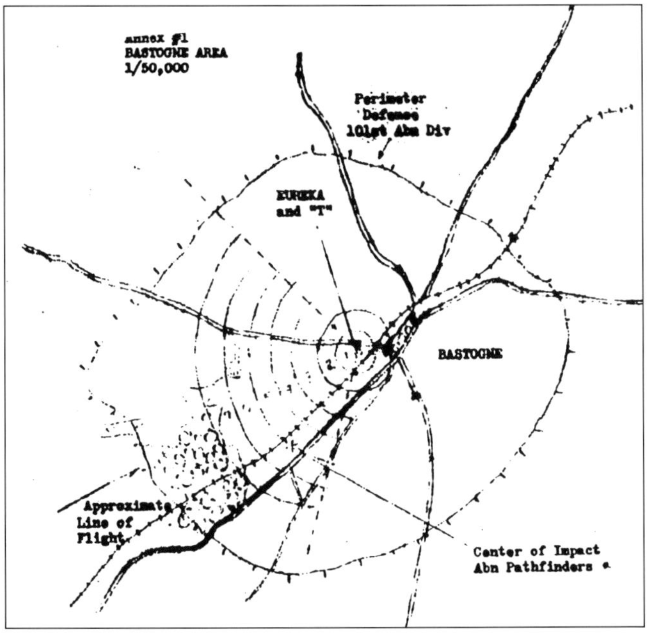

Map of the Bastogne resupply mission. *Author's Collection*

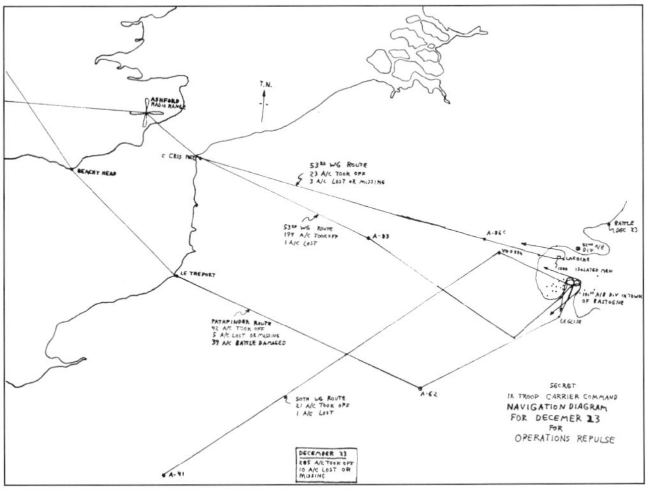

Navigation diagram for December 23 for Operation Repulse. *Author's Collection*

Sgt. John Agnew who parachuted in with one of the Eureka beacon sets picked out a spot on top of a pile of bricks to setup his set. This would help the signal for the incoming C-47s carrying vital supplies.

Of the total of 819 planes approximately thirty-two planes dropped their loads over enemy territory, unrecoverable.

Of the fifty gliders reported to have left England on the 27th of December thirty-three landed safely on the LZ. Three gliders were reported downed in enemy territory and were destroyed after landing.

Team '1', 506th Parachute Infantry Regiment, 101st Airborne Division

1 Lt. Schrable D. Williams	HQ	Team Leader
Sgt. James E. McNiece	HQ	
Sgt. John Mossman	A	
Sgt. Cleo Merz	C	
Sgt. Leroy E. Shulenberg	B	
Cpl. John W. Dewey	HQ	
T/5 George H. Blain	HQ	
Pfc. John Agnew	HQ	
Pvt. William E. Coad	HQ	
Pfc. George H, Slater	B	

Team '2', 506th Parachute Infantry Regiment, 101st Airborne Division

1 Lt. Gordon O. Rothwell	HQ
Cpl. Richard M. Wright	E
Cpl. Lavon P. Reese	E
Pfc. Carl L. Fenstermaker	E
Pvt. Lachman Tillman	D
Pvt. Charles H. Partlow	D
Pfc. Martin Majewski	HQ
Pfc. Mathon M. Forster	HQ
Pvt. Floyd Thomas	A
Pvt. Irvin L. Shumaker	H

Some of the Bastogne 101st Airborne Pathfinders in the Spring of 1945. Front Left to right: Cpl. Richard Wright, Pfc. Carl L. Fenstermaker, Sgt. Jake McNeice, T/5 George Blain; Rear Left to right: Lt. Schrable Williams, Pvt. Irvin L. Shumaker, Pfc. John Agnew, Pvt. Lachman Tillman, Pvt. Charles Partlow, Cpl. James Benson (didn't jump with the group into Bastogne, but jumped in the Prum resupply drop mission). *Courtesy of 101st Airborne Division Association*

PRUM, GERMANY - February 13, 1945

A team of pathfinders from the 506th Parachute Infantry Regiment, 101st Airborne Division were dropped in at Prum, Germany on February 13, 1945 in advance to direct the dropping of gasoline, rations, engineer equipment, and other supplies to the 4th Infantry Division. The division had overrun the town, but found itself cut off from its lines of communication by the Germans on one side and roads and bridges washed away be rains and an early thaw on the other. It became necessary to drop supplies to the division by air.

The mission to resupply them was called Operation Redball. It would consist of thirty-six aircraft from the 439th and forty aircraft from the 440th Troop Carrier Wings. The DZ was a 300x900 yards field near the Village of Bleialf, Germany, about seven miles East-Southeast of St. Vith, Germany.

The pathfinders successfully marked the DZ using M/F and Eureka beacons, red smoke and red signal panels, and green flares fired from a Very pistol.

A total of 486,705 pounds were successfully dropped. The first serials picked up the Eureka signal from 16 miles out and saw smoke ten miles away.

For a few of the pathfinders it was their fourth combat jump as pathfinders:

Sgt. James Benson operating his AN/PPN-1A Eureka beacon set in Prum, Germany. *Courtesy of 101st Airborne Division Association*

1 Lt. Schrable D. Williams	Regtl. HQ
Sgt. James Benson	
Pvt. Raymond Smith	502 PIR (medic)
T/5 George H. Blain	1 Bn.
Pvt. George Rhinehart	

RHINE CROSSING - March 24, 1945

The 17th Airborne Division formed one team of twelve men as pathfinders during the war. They were trained at Nottingham, England by veteran pathfinders of the 82nd and 101st after their return from Normandy. Some of the men were 2nd Lt. Richard Knight, S/Sgt. Curtis A. Gadd, Sgt. Charles Ust, Bill Dunsimore, Luther Davis, Mike Kmetz, and Irwin Paylor.

S/Sgt Curtis Gadd recalls, "We had 'volunteered' at Tidworth Barracks in England for this service after somewhat 'colorful' past performances. Somewhat like the 'dirty dozen'"

"We were shipped to Nottingham, England where they we met briefly with pathfinders from the 82nd and 101st after their return from Normandy. We were then shipped to Chalgrove Airbase, an 8th Air Force Base about twelve miles from Oxford for training in air to ground communications, panels, smoke, and the Eureka-Rebecca radar sets. The training took three months and was to be the best duty of our careers."

"We rejoined Company D of the 513th Para. Inf. Rgt. For the hurry up call for 'warm bodies' for the Battle of the Bulge. No pathfinders were needed."

It was decided for Operation Varsity, the airborne invasion of Germany, that pathfinders would not be dropped ahead of the airborne invasion because of the massive air armada converging from several airfields in Europe and England. The drop and landing zones were too heavily defended, and the drop of pathfinders ahead of incoming serials was considered 'suicidal'. The early presence of pathfinders would give away any element of surprise that might be left. Navigation to the DZs and LZs was not expected to any problem and because of the magnitude of the operation; the Pathfinder Group was needed to carry in airborne troops. They carried Col. Edson Raff and his 507th Parachute Infantry Regiment.

On 24 March 1945, pathfinders were however set up on the American held side of the Rhine River to help guide the 17th Airborne Division to its drop and landing zones near Wesel, Germany. This was the first time the AN/PPN-2 Eureka beacon was to be used in action during World War II.

Pathfinders and men of the 4th Armored open parachute bundles, this one containing grenades and rations. *Courtesy of Mark Bando*

One stick of pathfinders were to be in or near the lead of each serial heading for each DZ to set up signal panels and smoke. They took off at 0725 on 24 March from Chartres, France with the group commander, Col. Crouch as pilot and Col. Raff as a passenger. Airborne Divisions were to set up an M/F beacon on supply drop zones for resupply by B-24s following fifteen minutes behind the airborne armada. The LZs were not marked during the operation.

"If you read any accounts of that operation you will know that we were scattered all over Christ's creation. However, the operation has since been known as the largest and most successful airborne operation of the war."

This was the last large scale airborne operation used in the European Theater. So with the fighting coming to an end, the need for the large unit ceased to exist. They were soon to be disbanded.

Chapter Three

STATESIDE TRAINING

The 1st Troop Carrier Command established a Pathfinder School on September 1, 1944 for the training of its selected aircrews in pathfinder techniques. A month later the Army Air Force raised the question of moving the Troop Carrier Pathfinder Training Unit from Stout Field (Indianapolis, Indiana) to the North Carolina area in order to facilitate joint training with the airborne units at Camp Mackall. This fitted into the views of the airborne officers. They cooperated with the Troop Carrier Command in the preparation of training directives and drew up planes for a program of joint training. It was the proposal of the Airborne Center that joint training began on January 8, 1945 for twenty-five parachute pathfinder teams. The Pathfinder Division of the 1st Troop Carrier Command submitted a similar proposal for one month of joint training to be conducted at the Parachute School. A directive for joint training at the Airborne Center still was being prepared at the end of the month, and a week later the Troop Carrier Command received notice that pathfinder training was going to be discontinued.

In February 1944, the 541st Parachute infantry Battalion conducted several training jumps incorporating pathfinders at Camp Mackall, North Carolina. Various other units in the States also conducted similar training jumps with much success.

Chapter Four

11TH AIRBORNE DIVISION

The 11th Airborne Division was fighting the Japanese in the Pacific. One of its regiment, the 511th Parachute Infantry Regiment formed three pathfinder teams at Warrenburg Airfield in 1943. The three teams were comprised of men from the Regimental Headquarters Company of the 511th, with some of the men coming from the demolition platoon. They received three months of pathfinder training by personnel of the OSS.

The 511th Parachute Infantry Regiment was marshaled on Elmore and Hill airfields near San Jose, Mindoro, for the air assault, while their two glider regiments, the 187th and 188th, fought their way up Route 17 and into the Aga Defile.

The Regiment's pathfinder teams first mission, led by 1st Lt. David Hover, was to land by boat on the beach and slip through the enemy lines on February 1, 1945 and move up to Tagaytay Ridge carrying smoke pots to mark the drop zones.

On the morning of February 3, C-47s of Colonel John Lackey's 317th Troop Carrier Group took off from the Mindoro fields carrying the first echelon of the 511th. Lackey had only forty-eight C-47s available for the operation, enough to only carry one battalion of the regiment at a time. He planned to make two runs over the target, and to bring in the last battalion on the second day of the attack.

The sky was broken overcast as Lackey led his formation almost due north toward Luzon, where Lake Taal was his first checkpoint. He crossed the south shore of the lake at eight o'clock and angled off to the northeast, aiming at the high, mist-shrouded mount Sungay. The paratroops, peering out the jump doors on the left side of the aircraft, could watch their objective rising up dark blue at the north side of the lake.

When he could see Route 17, Lackey turned the formation back to the west, paralleling the road and heading in toward the rear of the Japanese positions. A column of white smoke rose from the drop zone far ahead, the pathfinders were in position. Lackey's first echelon of eighteen planes flew straight in to the drop zones and put 345 troopers out in the air precisely in the correct spot. The remaining echelons were not so lucky. As they began their run in to target, two door bundles were inadvertently knocked out of one of the first planes of the group. Some jumpmasters of other aircraft saw two parachutes opening and led their men out. The jump could not be stopped, and all the remaining thirty planes dropped their paratroopers almost five miles east of the objective. The planes were flying at twelve hundred feet, at a speed of 135 mile per hour. They had not slowed to the usual 110 miles per hour for the jump. The pathfinders were awarded Bronze Star medals for their participation in the operation.

On June 23, 1945, the major part of the 511th Regimental Combat Team operating as GYPSY Task Force conducted parachute and glider landings near Appari, a small seaport on the northern coast of Luzon. They were to prevent the Japanese from capturing the port. Pathfinders helped in the landings.

On June 21, 1945 the pathfinders of the 11th Airborne Division contacted Colonel Volckmann and his guerillas. On the night before the 511th drop, the pathfinders slipped across the Cagayan River and prepared the drop zone at Camalaniugan airfield near Appari.

The pathfinders popped green smoke at 0900 on June 23 to signal the task force. Winds over the drop zone area were 20-25 knots, and the terrain on the DZ was flooded with rice paddies, caribou wallows, bomb craters, and tall kunai grass. In 1947 the 11th Airborne would formally organize pathfinder teams.

Pathfinders of the 11th Airborne Division.

1 Lt. David Hover	PFC Joseph Rhinehart.
Frank Lloyd	(Others unknown)

Chapter Five

AIR CORPS PATHFINDERS

Near the end of the summer of 1943, numerous meetings were held in Comisco, Sicily, between Col. James Gavin of the 505th PIR, Lt.Col. Joel L. Crouch, Capt. Jack Norton S-3, 505th PIR, Capt. William S. Kirkpatrick from the 313th Troop Carrier Group, and Maj. B.L. 'Boy' Wilson, the commander of the British 21st Independent Parachute Company (Pathfinders). Maj. Wilson brought with him, and introduced to the Americans, the Rebecca-Eureka system.

At the meetings the idea for a Pathfinder School emerged and was developed. It was clearly established that the use of assigned drop zones, marked in advance of the main bodies of paratroops were need for future airborne operations. Even if the pathfinders missed their drop zones a little and the zones were improperly marked, that at least the main bodies of paratroopers would be dropped together, avoiding wide spread landings.

At first the Pathfinder School would train "one-mission-only" personnel. They would be assigned to the Pathfinder School on "temporary duty". Aircraft, equipment, and supplies were to be supplied to the school by the IX Troop Carrier Command. The aircrews were sent from the Groups of the 50th, 52nd, and 53rd Troop Carrier Wings then in the European Theater. The 82nd and 101st Airborne Divisions sent paratroopers to receive training in how to mark the drop and landing zones. A Pathfinder School was established in Cottesmore, England on February 28, 1944 with Lt.Col. Joel Crouch as the commander. On March 22, 1944 the school was moved to North Witham, England.

The men in the 9th Troop Carrier Command learned in late August of 1944, that a reorganization of top commands assigned them to the First Allied Airborne Army. To most, the only affect was a change of shoulder patches. The Ninth Air Force patch was replaced by a new one, with 'AIRBORNE' emblazoned across the top over 'TROOP CARRIER', and below that, a glider superimposed over an open parachute.

Some personnel of the 9th Troop Carrier had special patches made in local tailor shops in England. The word 'NINTH' was added above 'TROOP CARRIER'.

In September 1944 the Pathfinder School was moved and on the 14th the IX Troop Carrier Group (Provisional) was given the new designation of 1st Pathfinder Group – it was composed of four squadrons; 1st, 2nd, 3rd, and 4th. It made its last move on February 27, 1945 to Chartres, France. In July 1945, the pathfinders were inactivated. Both the pathfinders of the Air Corps and the Airborne returned to their parent units.

Pathfinders would again be formed in the U.S. Army for service during the Korean War and Vietnam War, and they would continue their service up to current time. Today all pathfinders are trained at their school in Ft. Benning, Georgia.

Col. Joel Crouch (Left) the commander of the Air Corps 9th Troop Carrier Pathfinder Group (Provisional) and Lt. Col. James T. Blair, Jr., XO, by their Headquarters sign in England I 1945. *Courtesy of the Air Force*

One of the C-47 aircrews of the 9th Troop Carrier Pathfinder Group that flew the Pathfinders to Normandy on June 6, 1944. *Courtesy of the Air Force*

Two at right - Top: U.S. made 9th Air Force patch with airborne tab above for personnel of the 9th Troop Carrier, worn before August 1944. Bottom: Troop Carrier Command patch worn after August 1944. *Author's Collection*

C-47 crew, which flew the lead plane on June 5, 1944. Standing Left to Right: Capt. Ray Culp (navigator), Lt. Col. Joel Crouch (pilot), Conrad (radio operator), Capt. Vito S. Pedone (co-pilot). Kneeling Left to Right: Doctor E. Cannon (group flight surgeon), Sgt. E. Laurendeal (crew chief). *Courtesy of the Air Force*

Chapter Six

INSIGNIA

The idea of a special insignia for the pathfinders was envisioned in May 1944. The men in the pathfinders were volunteers and professionals and were specialist in a unique field, which would justify a special insignia. One of the group's navigators, Lt. Prescott, and gifted at drawing, was asked to help with its design and put in charge.

The final design was submitted to Lt.Col. Crouch and approved. The flaming winged torch became the distinctive insignia of the Pathfinders. Lt. Prescott immediately went to an insignia maker in London where he had the first lot made.

Coincidence or not, the first lot arrived to the unit on the morning of June 5, 1944, just in time for the invasion of Normandy. Some personnel had the new insignia sewn on their uniforms so they could be worn during the invasion. But, that was not liked by superior officers who visited the group before the flight, because if the individual wearing it was captured, German Intelligence would want to know its meaning. Since it was still a fairly new and secret unit, they felt it would draw unwanted attention. Lt.Col. Crouch stood up for his men and told the officers that to make them take off the insignia would make them have a lack of confidence. Nevertheless it was decided that from then on the insignia would only be worn on the dress uniform. The wearing of the insignia in combat was forbidden.

Both the paratroops and aircrews alike were entitled to wear the insignia. To earn the patch you did not have to be involved in a 'combat' operation, you only had to have completed the training. Foreign troops who completed training in the various pathfinder schools setup during the war were also entitled to wear it. It is believed that the only non-American unit to obtain the privilege of wearing the winged torch Pathfinder insignia was the British 1st Independent Parachute Platoon in recognition of the 150 days they spent in Sicily to train the U.S. 51st Troop Carrier Wing.

The original flaming winged torch insignia was embroidered on a piece of dark purple wool approximately 2.5 x 3 inches and was then trimmed down to the shape of the wing and torch, leaving only a small border. It was sewn on the lower left sleeve with the torch end on the downward angle above the service stripes. (It was however sewn at many different angles leaning forward or backward).

Many variations exist of the insignia, most notably a later version made by the same London maker as the first except on dark blue wool, and were made in both a flat and padded version. Other variations had slightly different colors and were various sizes. Some of the more notable private purchase variations were hand embroidered, bullion embroidered, and an English made version which was hand embroidered on dark red wool – no reason for this unique version is known. In the mid-1980s, a pathfinder reenactment group in the U.S. had a British style wing on maroon backing made (they are not original).

I have seen more than twenty-two variations of the insignia. One man having one made downtown or making it himself constitutes a variation. Original pathfinder insignia are extremely rare today and reproductions of the insignia are sometimes difficult to tell from originals.

The pathfinder wing was later approved in 1952 by the Department of Heraldry and is still worn by trained pathfinders today, although it is made differently and no longer worn on the sleeve. It is now worn on the left upper pocket.

British made Pathfinder wing on uncut dark blue felt. *Courtesy of Bill Rentz*

British made wing on uncut blue felt. *Courtesy of Michel De Trez*

Pathfinder wing on uncut dark blue felt. *Author's Collection*

British made wing on dark blue felt. *Author's Collection*

Large 1945 pathfinder pocket patch which could be purchased from the PX. *Author's Collection*

British made bullion private purchase wing. *Author's Collection*

Below: British made wing worn on the British made ETO jacket of a Master Sergeant of the 505th Para. Inf. Regt., 82nd Abn. Div. *Courtesy of Bill Rentz*

Above: British made wing being worn by S/Sgt. Berge Avadanian of the 505th Para. Inf. Regt., 82nd Abn. Div. *Courtesy of Berge Avadanian*

Above right: Pvt. Frank 'Vic' Hudon of the 504th Para. Inf. Regt., 82nd Abn. Div. He was a pathfinder of the Salerno jump in 1943 and the Holland jump in 1944. This picture was taken shortly after his return to the USA. *Courtesy of Vic Hudon*

Right: Pfc. Henry J. Hirlemann, a pathfinder of the 325th Glider Inf. Regt, 82nd Abn. Div. jumped in the Holland operation in Sept. 1944. *Courtesy of Henry Hirlmann*

1st Lt. James J. Smith, the pathfinder team leader for the 2nd Bn, 505th Para. Inf. Regt. for the Normandy invasion. *Courtesy of 82nd Airborne Museum, Ft. Bragg, NC*

This is the four-pocket jacket was worn by Sgt. Gerald Shaw, a medic with the 504th Para. Inf. Regt., 82nd Abn. Div. He was a qualified pathfinder and participated in the Holland drop on September 17, 1944. He helped mark Drop Zone 'O'. He wears the combat medic badge on the center of the upper left pocket and a pathfinder wing on dark blue on the lower left sleeve in the correct manor. *Courtesy of Ben Overhand*

Sgt. Shaw wears the combat medical badge in the center of his pocket. *Courtesy of Ben Overhand*

Left: His pathfinder wing is very closely trimmed. *Courtesy of Ben Overhand*

Right: Sgt. Shaw wearing an "Ike" jacket at the end of the war. *Courtesy of Ben Overhand*

This "Ike" jacket is from a Master Sergeant who served as a pathfinder in the 505th Para. Inf. Regt., 82nd Abn. Div. *Courtesy of Bill Rentz*

Left: Close-up detail shows the British made jump wings with four campaign stars and an invasion arrowhead attached to a British made 505th background. The ribbons are mounted on felt over a British made embroidered Combat Infantry badge. Right: Felt pathfinder wing worn with the popular cross-stitch pattern over British made hash marks for two years overseas duty. *Courtesy of Bill Rentz*

Right: The "Ike" jacket worn by Pathfinder Pvt. Mathew Kantala of Co. I, 504th Para. Inf. Regt., 82nd Abn. He made the Waal River crossing where he was wounded. *Courtesy of Ben Overhand*

Above left: Closer view of his awards. The orange lanyard was awarded for the Holland Operation. Above right: Closer view of his British made wing. *Courtesy of Ben Overhand*

This "Ike" jacket was worn by Cpl. Ralph E. Haines of the 82nd Abn. Div. Below: The pathfinder wing is a British made on blue felt. *Author's Collection*

Right: S/Sgt. Dan Mason's "Ike" jacket showing the pathfinder wing and jump wings with four stars and an arrowhead. *Courtesy of Dudley Cone*

Left: S/Sgt. Dan Mason a pathfinder of the 505th Parachute Infantry Regiment won the Silver Star in Sicily. He trained as a pathfinder but never jumped with them. Right: Close up view of the pathfinder wing worn on S/Sgt. Mason's Ike jacket. *Courtesy of Dudley Cone*

Left: Pfc. Gilbert Gamely was a pathfinder of the 505th Parachute Infantry Regiment, like all pathfinders who jumped into Normandy he was awarded the Bronze Star for his participation. Above: Pfc. Gamely with two unknown troopers in England. *Courtesy of Dudley Cone*

Pfc. Gamely's "Ike" jacket showing his pathfinder wing. Below: Pfc. Gamely's pathfinder wing. *Courtesy of Dudley Cone*

Right: This "Ike" jacket worn by 1st Lt. Gordon Deramus, of the 502nd. He was the team leader of the 101st pathfinder team three assigned to mark Drop Zone 'B' for the Holland operation on September 17, 1944. He has an English made pathfinder wing worn in the correct manor on lower left sleeve above overseas hash marks for two years. He also has 502nd regimental numbered officers infantry collar brass, a Belgium foraguerre on right shoulder, and Holland orange lanyard for the 'Market Garden' operation. Right: Closer view of the pathfinder wing. *Courtesy of Michel De Trez*

Ike jacket worn by S/Sgt. Edward McNair, who was a pathfinder for the 101st Airborne Division and winner of the Silver Star. Near the war's end, he transferred to the 11th Airborne Division for the duration of the war. Below: On the right cuff sleeve he has a Theater made pathfinder wing over four bold bullion Theater made hash marks for two years of overseas duty. *Courtesy of Bill Rentz*

Right: This is the "Ike" jacket worn by S/Sgt. Curtis A. Gadd of D Company 513th Para. Inf. Regt., 17th Abn. Div. He 'volunteered' to be a pathfinder in 1944 at Tidworth Barracks in England. *Courtesy of Curtis Gadd*

This officers garrison cap and "Ike" jacket belonged to Capt. A. Lazzoni of the 509th Para. Inf. Bn. Note the British bullion jump wings above the right pocket and green leaders tabs. On his right shoulder he wears a Theater made 509th patch. Bottom left: Closer view of the theater made pathfinder wing. *Author's Collection*

Above: S/Sgt. Bill Lumsden a pathfinder of the 551st Para. Inf. Bn. who jumped into Southern France on the night of August 15, 1944. Photo taken in early 1943 on leave after he returned from Panama. *Courtesy of Bill Lumsden*

Right: This dress uniform was worn by S/Sgt. Boyer of the 9th Troop Carrier Command. He was a crew chief of one of the C-47 transport aircraft. He wears the Army Air Corps patch on the right shoulder. *Author's Collection*

Right: View of the English made 9th Troop Carrier Command patch. *Author's Collection*

Far right: Closer view of the British made pathfinder wing worn by S/Sgt. Boyer. *Author's Collection*

This British made "Ike" jacket was worn by Capt. Leonard E. Reed, the Engineering officer of the 74th Troop Carrier Squadron. After Normandy there was a shortage of Glider pilots so he volunteered and earned his glider wings in England. He was then attached to the IX Troop Carrier Pathfinder Group. The war ended before he made any combat flights. *Courtesy of Bill Rentz*

Closer view of the closely trimmed pathfinder wing. *Courtesy of Bill Rentz*

Below: The glider wings and ribbon bar are British made. He wears the Troop Carrier patch on his right shoulder. *Courtesy of Bill Rentz*

Officers service dress uniform belonging to Capt. Leonard E. Reed 74th Troop Carrier Squadron. Note the pin-back Technical Observer wings. *Courtesy of Bill Rentz*

Closely trimmed pathfinder patch worn by Capt. Reed. *Courtesy of Bill Rentz*

IKE jacket worn by a Sgt. of the 8th Air Force. He was a formerly a pathfinder with the Troop Carrier Command. The British made wing is worn over hash marks for 2 1/2 years overseas duty. *Author's Collection*

Left
Top: He wears an 'AIRBORNE' tab over the 8th Air Force patch on his left shoulder.

Middle: Closer view of the Troop Carrier patch worn on the right shoulder.

Bottom: View of the British made pathfinder wing. *Author's Collection*

1st Pathfinder Group patch made for the pathfinders who trained at the 5th Army Airborne Training Center prior to Operation Dragoon, the Invasion of Southern France on August 14-15, 1944. The patch was designed by and made for them selves. *Courtesy of L.Hughes*

Below

Left: Pfc. Henry A. Ciner was a pathfinder of the 517th Para. Inf. Regt who jumped in the Southern France invasion on August 14, 1944. He was killed in action on Aug. 15 near LeMuy, France. Photo taken in Oct. 1943 after his graduation from Airborne School. *Courtesy of MacLean Lunko*

Right: Pfc. Ciner after his graduation from Airborne School. *Courtesy of MacLean Lunko*

Above: Robert D. Hopping a pathfinder in the 517th Parachute Infantry Regiment. Photo taken after his graduation from Jump School. *Courtesy of Melissa Kramer*

Left: Sgt. Milton "Fuzzy" V. Knight of HQ, 1st BN., 504th Parachute Infantry Regiment, 82nd Airborne Division. Picture taken in Sicily, 1943. *Courtesy of Ben Overhand*

Below: Robert Hopping with his son Robert Hopping, Jr. *Courtesy of Milissa Kramer*

Chapter Seven

UNIFORMS

During World War II, American Pathfinders wore four basic uniforms, two for dress occasions and one each for training and combat. The two uniforms worn for dress occasions were the class-A four-pocket, and later short 'Ike' jacket with shirt, tie, and trousers bloused over the jump boots (both uniform styles can be seen in chapter six).

For training and combat they first wore the Model 1942 jump suit, which consisted of a jacket and pants made from a lightweight cotton twill in various shades of tan. During the Salerno operation the men of the 504th and 505th Para. Inf. Regts. wore their 82nd Abn. Div. patch sewn to the left shoulder and a small U.S. flag printed on gauze sewn to the right sleeve.

Many of the pathfinders who jumped into Salerno carried their special equipment strapped to their legs by means of the British designed leg bag.

A few weeks prior to the Normandy invasion paratroops of the 82nd and 101st Airborne Divisions turned in one jump suit to their division's riggers to be reinforced with heavy waterproof olive drab canvas. The elbows, and lower pockets of the jackets and the knees and leg cargo pockets of the pants were reinforced with the canvas material. Tie straps were also added to the legs to hold equipment tightly to the wearer. Slight variations in the way the jump suits were reinforced can be seen and are discussed in several books.

In the days prior to the invasion many of the pathfinders from both the 82nd and 101st painted their jump suits with various shades of green and black paint which they could scrounge or get from the aircrews. The divisional shoulder insignia, any rank chevrons, and the small U.S. flags the 82nd wore on their upper right arm were also painted over. Some of their equipment was also painted. The purpose of painting their suits and equipment was for a camouflage effect as they would be parachuting in the early morning darkness on the first day of the invasion and their tan jump suits could easily be seen in the darkness making easy targets for the Germans.

Some members of the 82nd pathfinder teams also painted one of the jackets cuffs with M5 vesicant gas detection paint. Many pathfinders of the 101st wore the gas detection brassard around one of their upper arms.

Men of the 101st painted white symbols on the sides of their jump helmets for help in identification purposes, various regiments, battalions, and companies having different symbols. The pathfinders of the division left their parent units to train in isolation in Nottingham some time before the stencils were applied. The security personnel were assigned less than two weeks before the invasion and brought their stenciled helmets with them. The men of the 82nd also had painted symbols on their helmets but it is not known if the pathfinders had these done. Equipment was often altered or made by divisional riggers; ammunition pouches, shovel handles shortened, straps added, etc.

Like the pathfinders in the Normandy invasion the paratroops and pathfinders who would participate in the Southern France operation also painted their jump suits and some equipment. A few days prior to the invasion, a detachment of engineers was detailed to camouflage clothing and equipment for the paratroops. Each man would file through a paint spray line, wearing his uniform with a cardboard box over his head. They were painted with shades of green and black oil paint. Equipment was either worn or laid to the side to be painted. Like the 82nd Airborne for the Normandy invasion U.S. flags were sewn on the left sleeve of their jackets.

The M42 jump suits were later replaced by the standard M1943 field jacket and pants. They were made from a heavier water resistant dark green cotton poplin material. Prior to Operation Market Garden, the paratroops of the 82nd and 101st had large cargo pockets made from dark green canvas added to the outside legs of the pants. Leg tie straps were also added as on the earlier M42 jump pants. Men of both divisions had small U.S. flags sewn to the upper right arm. Many of the flags were cut from the oilcloth flag armbands, which had been issued for the Normandy landings.

When the pathfinders of the 511th Parachute Infantry Regiment, 11th Airborne Division went ashore for the Tagaytay Ridge mission on February 3, 1945 they wore either the M42 Jump suit or the second style herringbone twill (HBT) shirt and trousers. It was the wearer's discretion as to which uniform he wore. He also wore either the jump boots or two buckle combat boots, which were standard army issue in the later part of the war.

This jump suit is heavily camouflaged with blobs of green tone paint. The elbows and knees have leather patches added for reinforcement. Nylon parachute strapping has been added to reinforce the cargo pockets. This particular method of reinforcing was done by the 504th during the early days. *Courtesy of Michel De Trez*

M-2 D-ring version paratroop helmet painted with three tone splotch paint which was done for the Sicily operation. *Courtesy of Michel De Trez*

Equipment carried by the pathfinder which has been camouflaged with green paint and modified by having extra magazine pouches added to shovel cover and carbine jump case. The handle of the shovel has also been shortened. *Courtesy of Michel De Trez*

A pathfinder of the 504th Parachute Infantry Regiment, 82nd Airborne Division. Twenty-six volunteers from the 504th jumped with the pathfinder teams of the 507th and 508th Regiments in the Normandy invasion. *Courtesy of Michel De Trez*

This is the M42 jump suit that was worn by a pathfinder of the 505th. It has been camouflaged with one tone green brush-paint and impregnated with a malodorous chemical to resist both water and gas. On the right sleeve is sewn the small cloth version of the American flag. The left sleeve has his patch of his division, the 82nd Airborne. The right cuff is painted with M5 vesicant detector paint, which reacted visibly in the presence of poison gases. *Courtesy of Michel De Trez*

M-2 D-ring paratroop helmet which is camouflaged in gas detection paint. This was particular for the men of the 505th who participated in the Sicily operation in 1943. *Courtesy of Michel De Trez*

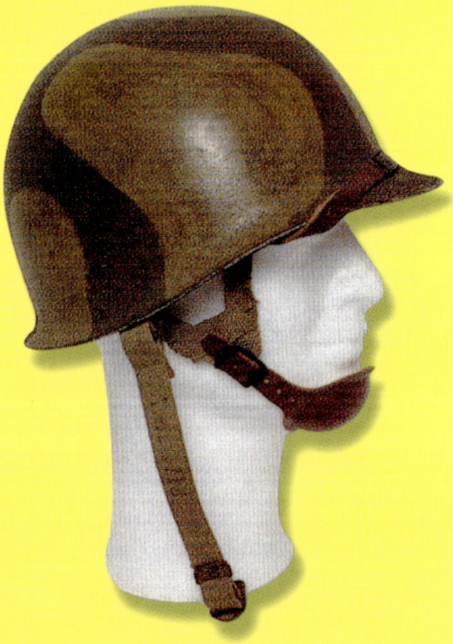

Equipment worn by a pathfinder of the 82nd Airborne. Once again the shovel handle has been shortened and the jump rope has been heavily camouflage painted. *Courtesy of Michel De Trez*

A pathfinder of the 505th Parachute Infantry Regiment, 82nd Airborne Division as he would appear for the Normandy invasion on June 6, 1944. *Courtesy of Michel De Trez*

A pathfinder of the 377th Parachute Field Artillery Battalion, 101st Airborne Division as he would appear for the Normandy invasion on June 6, 1944. He carries a signal light and three signal panels in the special carrying case behind his reserve parachute pack. He is armed with a M1928A-1 Thompson submachine gun, Hawkins anti-tank mine on his left leg, and M-3 trench knife on his right leg. *Author's Collection*

Left: Pvt. Charles Petty a pathfinder of the 509th Parachute Infantry Battalion jumped in the Southern France operation, with the M42 jump jacket he wore during the operation shown above. *Courtesy of Michel De Trez*

Top left: An Engineer spray-painting a paratrooper's M43 field jacket and pants. Notice the added pockets added by the riggers to his pants and the cardboard box worn over his head. *Courtesy of Michel De Trez*

A Pathfinder of the 509th Parachute Infantry battalion with a Holophane light, CS-150 case for signal panels on his right side, and a Griswold case for his weapon on his left side. *Courtesy of Michel Detrez*

Below: A Pathfinder Corporal of the 82nd Airborne Division laying out a bright red signal panel on the drop zone in Holland on September 17, 1944. *Author's Collection*

A Pathfinder of the 505th Parachute Infantry Regiment, 82nd Airborne Division upon his return to the United States after VE Day in 1945. He is a veteran of the Salerno, Normandy, and Holland landings. *Author's Collection*

BIBLIOGRAPHY

Books

Ambrose, Stephen E., *Band of Brothers*, Simon and Schuster, 1993.

Andrews, John, *Airborne Album*, Phillips Publications, Inc., 1981.

Astor, Gerald, *Battling Buzzards*, Donald I. Books, 1993.

Bando, Mark A., *The 101st Airborne at Normandy*, Motorbooks International, 1994.

Bando, Mark A., *The 101st Airborne from Holland to Hitler's Eagle's Nest*, Motorbooks International, 1995.

Breuer, William B., *Operation Dragoon*, Berkley Publishing Group, 1988

Breuer, William B., *Geronimo*, St. Martin's Press, 1989.

Crookenden, Napier, *Drop Zone Normandy*, Charles Scribners, 1976.

De Trez, Michel, *American Warriors*, D-Day Publishing, 1994.

De Trez, Michel, *At the Point of No Return*, D-Day Publishing, 1994.

De Trez, Michel, *First Airborne Task Force*, D-Day Publishing 1998.

Devlin, Gerald M., *Paratrooper*, St. Martin's Press, 1979.

Howard, Gary, *America's Finest*, Stackpole Books, 1994.

Morgan, Dan, *The Left Corner of my Heart*, Alder, 1984.

Rapport, Leonard and Northwood, Arthur, *Rendezvous with Destiny*, 101st Airborne Division Association, 1948.

Rentz, Bill, *Geronimo*, Schiffer Publishing Ltd, 1999.

Ryan, Cornelious, *The Longest Day*, Simon and Schuster, 1959.

Shama, H. Rex, *Pulse and Repulse*, Eakin Press, 1995.

Young, Charles H., *Into The Valley,* PrintComm, Inc., 1995.

Reports and Papers

505th Parachute Infantry, 82nd Airborne Division After Action Report, Cpt. John Norton.

508th Parachute Infantry Regiment Pathfinders for Normandy – June 5, 1994, Bob Weaver.

Government Order #39 504 PIR Personnel who Volunteered as Pathfinders for Operation Neptune

(Normandy) – Award of the Bronze Star, 21 July 1994.

Letter of Transmittal – Operation Market, 18 Dec. 1944, Lt Col James T. Blair.

My Experiences of Rolland Duff in Europe.

Reflections of War: Experiences with the 325th Glider Infantry Regiment, 82nd Airborne Division in WWII

May 1989, Erwin Kitchenmaster.

Report of Airborne Pathfinder Operation 'Nuts', 7 Jan 1945, Cpt, Frank Brown.

Report of Pathfinder Employment for Operation 'Neptune' 11 June 1944 Cpt N. L. Mc Roberts.

Report of Pathfinder Mission, Operation Market, 30 November 1944, 1 Lt. J. Wifred Jaubert.

The Operations of a Regimental Pathfinder Unit, 507th Parachute Infantry Regiment, (82nd Airborne Division) in Normandy, France, 6 June 1944.

The Operations of a Regimental Pathfinder Unit, Cpt. John T. Joseph.

ALSO FROM THE PUBLISHER

THE ALL AMERICAN
An Illustrated History of the 82nd Airborne Division
1917 – to the Present
Robert P. Anzuoni

This new book tells the complete story of the famous 82nd Airborne Division from its formation in 1917, through its legendary World War II campaigns (Sicily, Normandy and Holland), Vietnam, Grenada, Nicaragua, Operation Desert Storm to the present, and examines the many changes from a World War I infantry division to the rapid deployment organization it is today.
Size: 8 1/2" x 11" • over 230 b/w, color photographs • 176 pp.
ISBN: 0-7643-1321-5 • hard cover • $45.00

U.S. ARMY RANGERS & SPECIAL FORCES
of World War II • Their War in Photographs
Robert Todd Ross

During World War II the United States Army organized a remarkable array of highly specialized, small units. The ranks of these forces were filled with men who, by virtue of their natural aggressiveness and intensive training, possessed diverse war-making skills well beyond those of standard troops. This book, by the author of *The Supercommandos*, tells the story of the U.S. Army's elite Rangers and Special Forces largely through pictures. Never before has such an expansive view of World War II elite forces been offered in one volume. An extensive search of public and private archives unearthed an astonishing number of rare and never before seen images, including color. Most notable are the nearly twenty exemplary photographs of Lieutenant Colonel William O. Darby's Ranger Force in Italy, taken by Robert Capa, considered by many to be the greatest combat photographer of all time. Complementing the period photographs are numerous color plates detailing the rare and often unique items of insignia, weapons, and equipment that marked the soldiers whose heavy task it was to "Lead the Way."
Size: 8 1/2" x 11" • over 250 black and white and color photographs • 216 pp.
ISBN: 0-7643-1682-6 • hard cover • $59.95

THE SUPERCOMMANDOS:
FIRST SPECIAL SERVICE FORCE
1942-1944 • An Illustrated History
Robert Todd Ross

Chronicles the organization, training, and combat operations of the First Special Service Force during its brief but exhilarating history. Full-color maps, Order of Battle graphics, charts, and numerous noteworthy original Force documents are also included. Over eighty full-color images of authentic First Special Service Force uniforms, insignia, weapons and equipment. An invaluable resource for any collector, reenactor, veteran, or historian.
Size: 8 1/2" x 11" • over 600 b/w photographs, over eighty color photographs, maps, documents • 320 pp
ISBN: 0-7643-1171-9 • hard cover • $59.95

THE SKY MEN
A Parachute Rifle Company's Story of the Battle of the Bulge and the Jump Across the Rhine
Kirk B. Ross

This is the story of F Company of the 513th Parachute Infantry Regiment, 17th U.S. Airborne Division. They were all volunteers to a new, dangerous, and elite corps – Airborne. Includes many never before used documents, with the personal accounts of nearly one hundred men of F Company and other associated organizations.
Size: 6" x 9" • over 130 b/w photographs, documents, maps • 544 pp.
ISBN: 0-7643-1172-7 • hard cover • $35.00

GERONIMO!
U.S. Airborne Uniforms, Insignia & Equipment
in World War II
Bill Rentz

Explores the uniforms, insignia, and equipment of American Airborne, Glider, Troop Carrier, and Airborne Engineers in World War II. Detailed images of individual items, multi-side views of full combat rig, and over 100 World War II photos, most unpublished, showing the uniforms and equipment as worn by the troops. Also a comparative section with both British and German airborne gear. An important reference work for the airborne collector, reenactor, historian and veteran.
Size: 9" x 12" • over 630 color and b/w photos • 192 pp.
ISBN: 0-7643-0677-4 • hard cover • $59.95

THE M-1 HELMET
A History of the U.S. M-1 Helmet in World War II
Mark A. Reynosa

Presents over seven years of research into the history of the M-1 helmet during World War II, and provides the most comprehensive examination of its development and production. All aspects of M-1 helmet production are covered, and every production helmet version is presented in full color photographs, including detail shots and production markings. Also included are era photographs of the helmet samples, helmet production, and helmets worn in training or in action. This book is a valuable reference to historians and collectors.
Size: 8 1/2" x 11" • 350+ color and b/w photos • 112 pp.
ISBN: 0-7643-0074-1 • hard cover • $39.95

FOR KING AND COUNTRY
British Airborne Uniforms, Insignia & Equipment
in World War II • 1st Airborne Division • 6th Airborne Division • 1st Polish Independent Parachute Brigade
Harlan Glenn

The first in a series of in-depth studies which will cover the uniforms, equipment, insignia, weapons, vehicles, and personal items of the British and Commonwealth soldier of World War II. This initial volume covers the British Airborne soldier of the 1st and 6th Airborne Divisions, and the 1st Polish Independent Parachute Brigade. An essential reference for any military enthusiast, collector, reenactor, and modeler.
Size: 9" x 12" • over 600 color and b/w photographs • 192 pp.
ISBN: 0-7643-0794-0 • hard cover • $59.95

GERMAN PARATROOPS
Uniforms, Insignia & Equipment of the Fallschirmjäger
in World War II
Robert Kurtz

The uniforms and equipment of the elite German Fallschirmjäger is the subject of this detailed, illustrated study. Authentic items – smocks, dress tunics, boots, insignia, helmets, visor caps, gloves, knee pads and more – are shown in superb color photos. Unpublished World War II era photos show uniforms and equipment being worn on a variety of war fronts. Also included is a short chapter covering other Axis airborne.
Size: 9" x 12" • over 300 color and b/w photographs • 192 pp.
ISBN: 0-7643-1040-2 • hard cover • $59.95